GABRIEL JONES

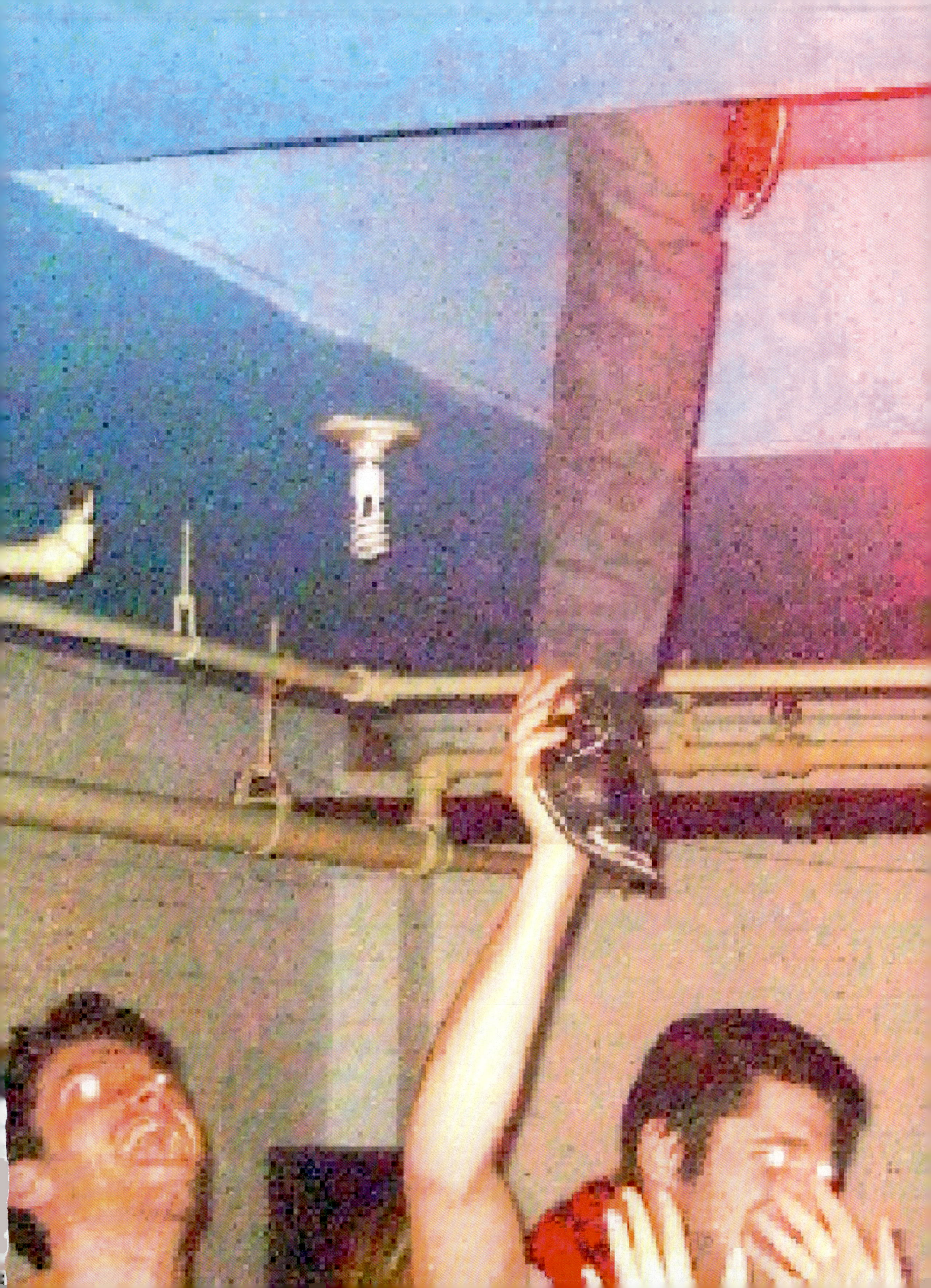

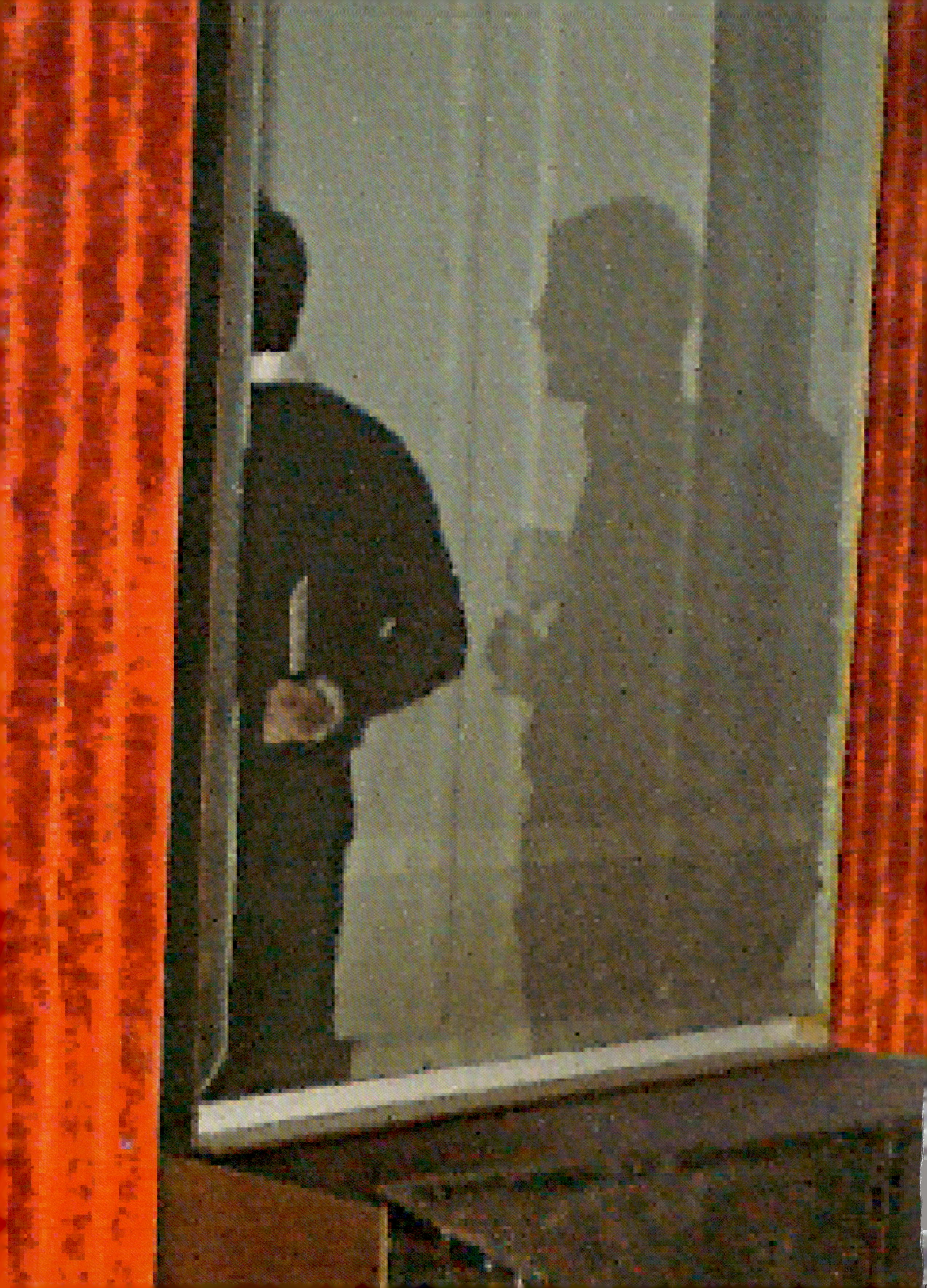

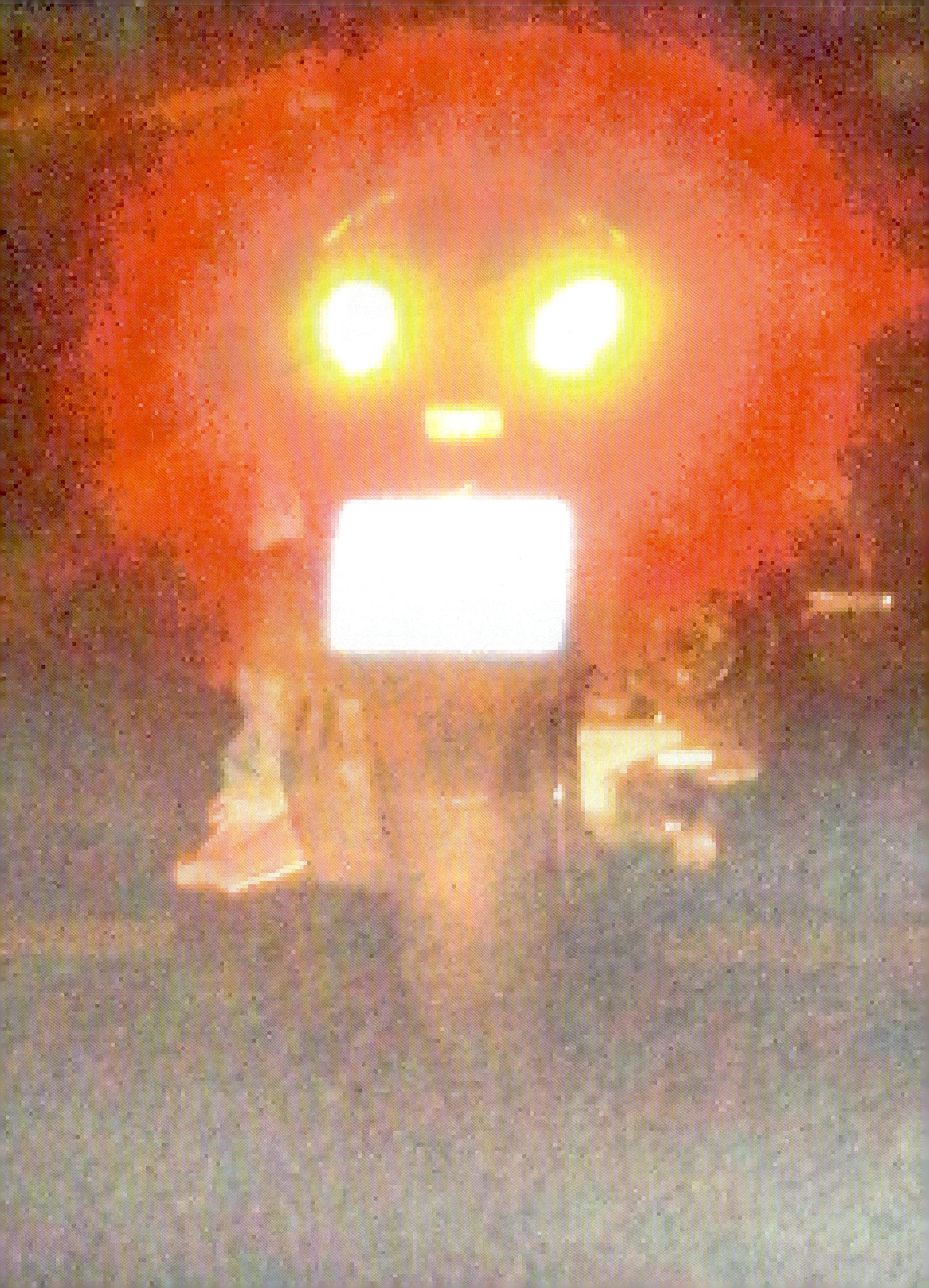

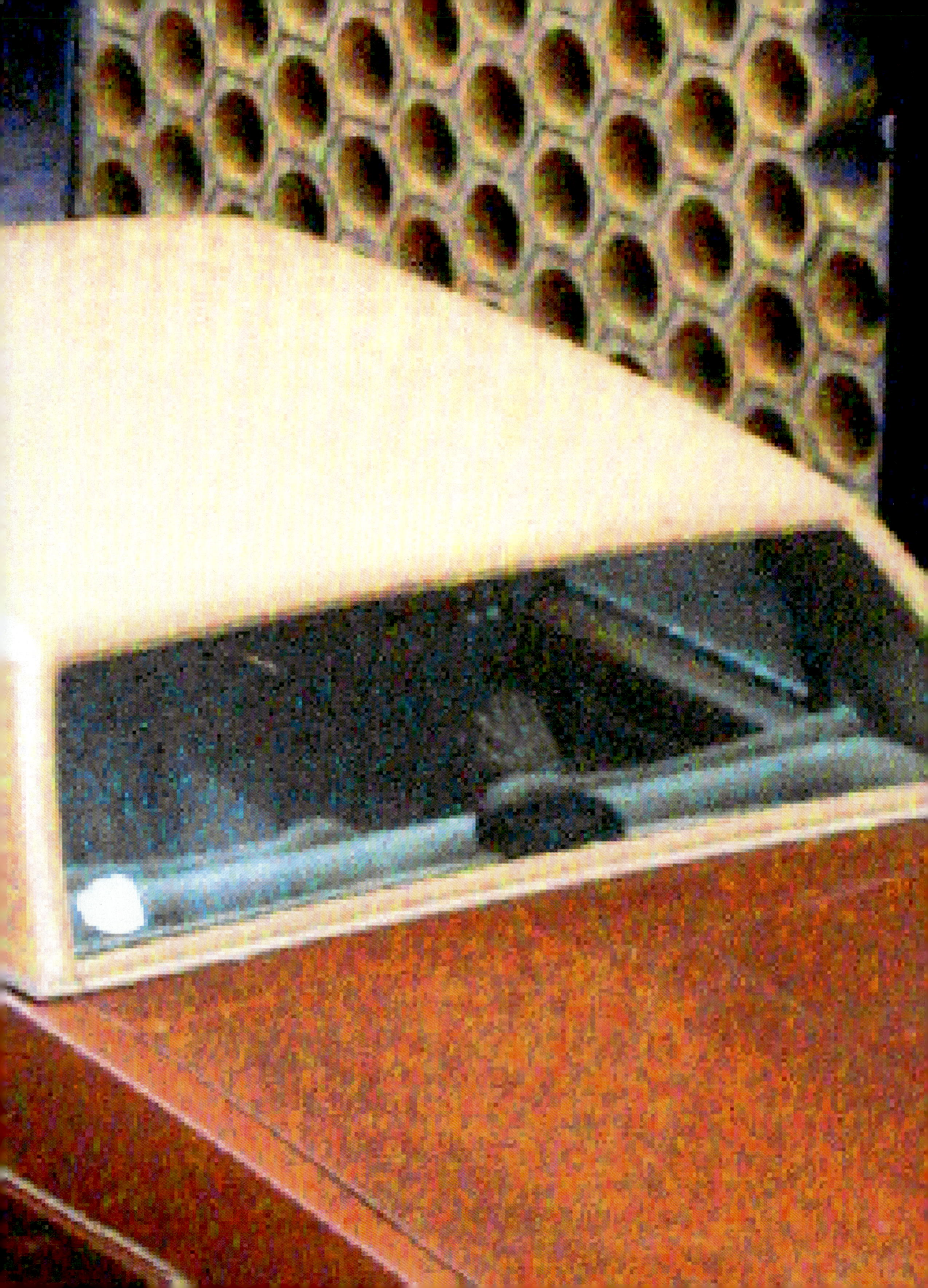

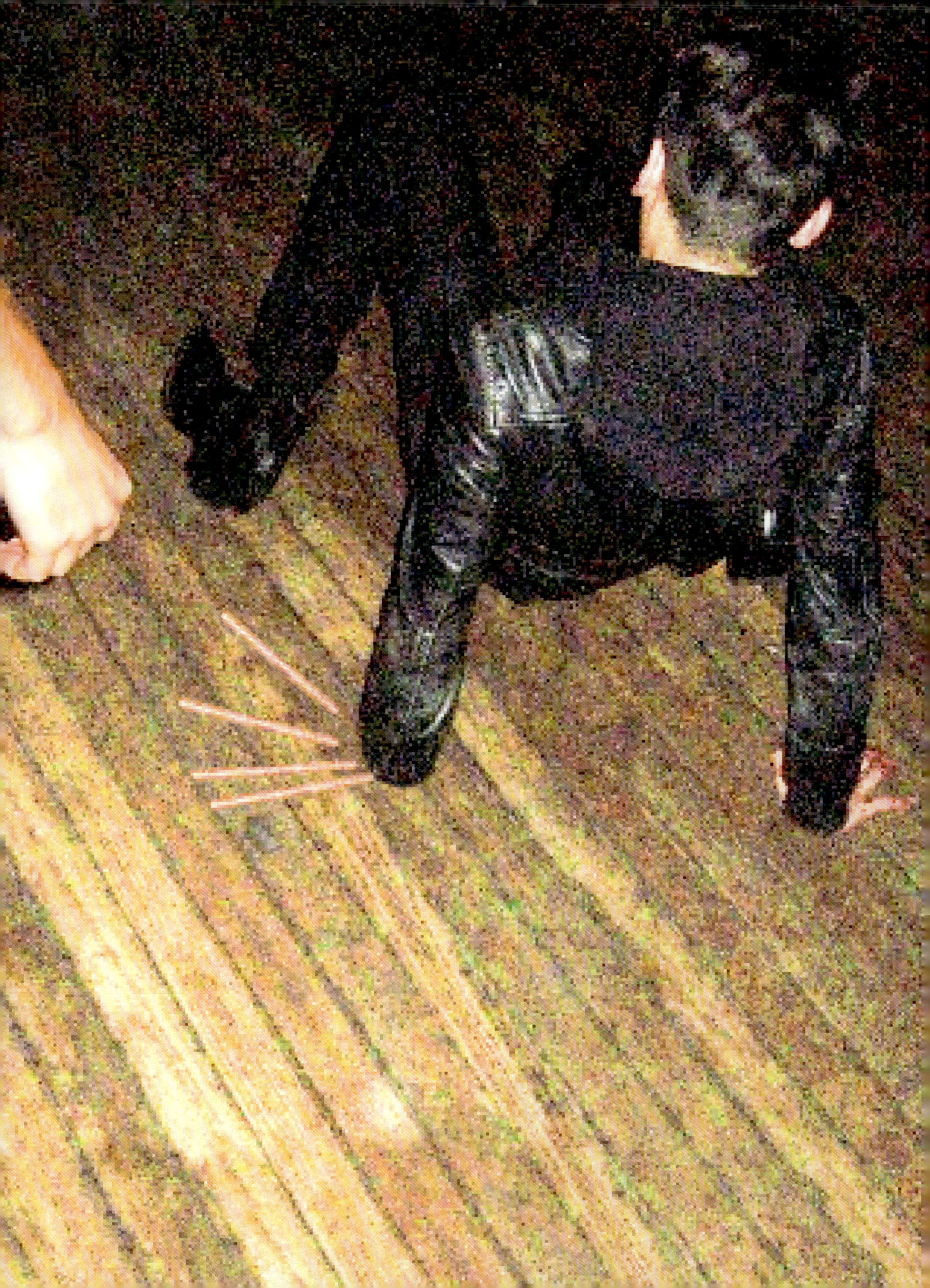

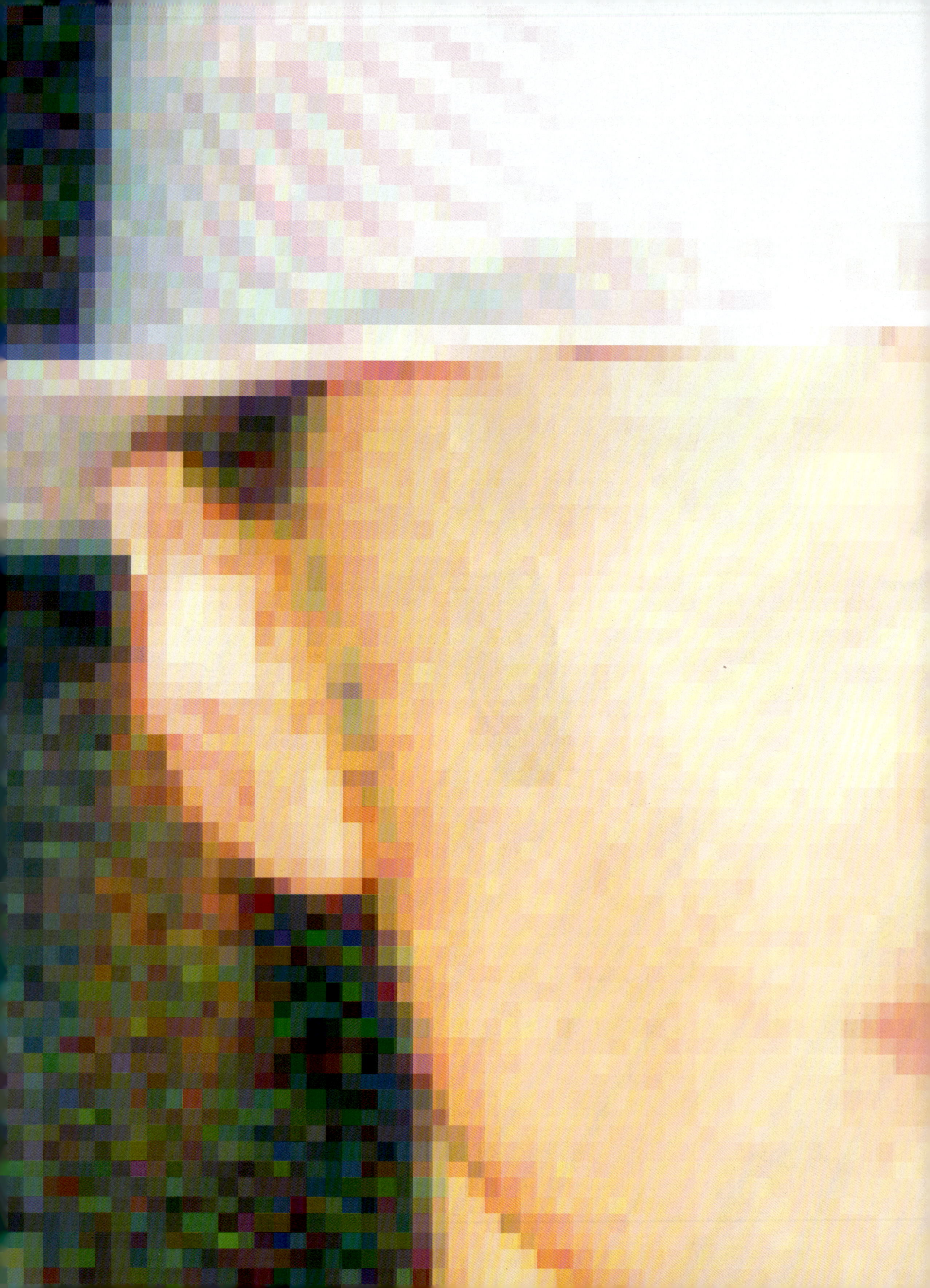

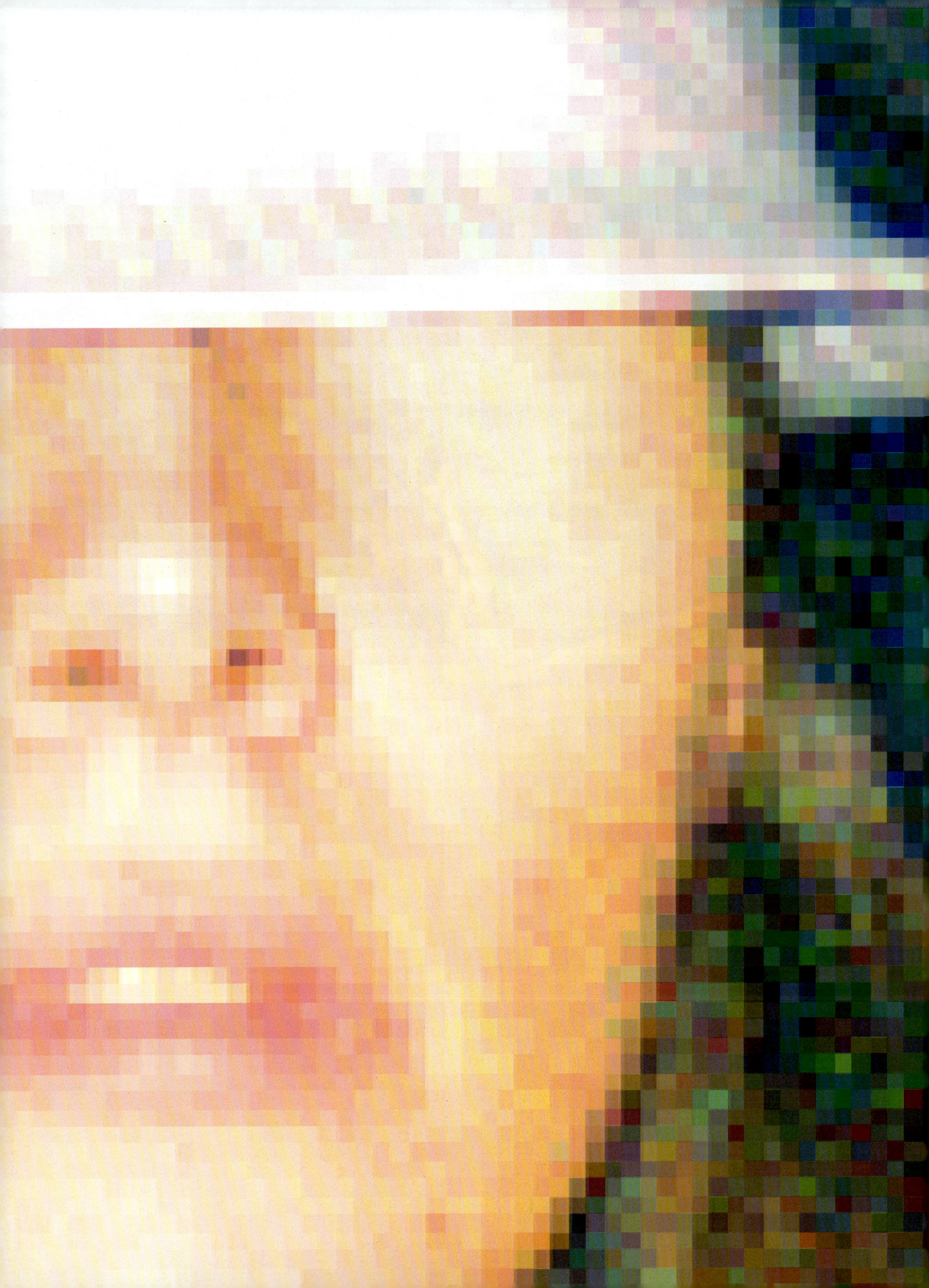

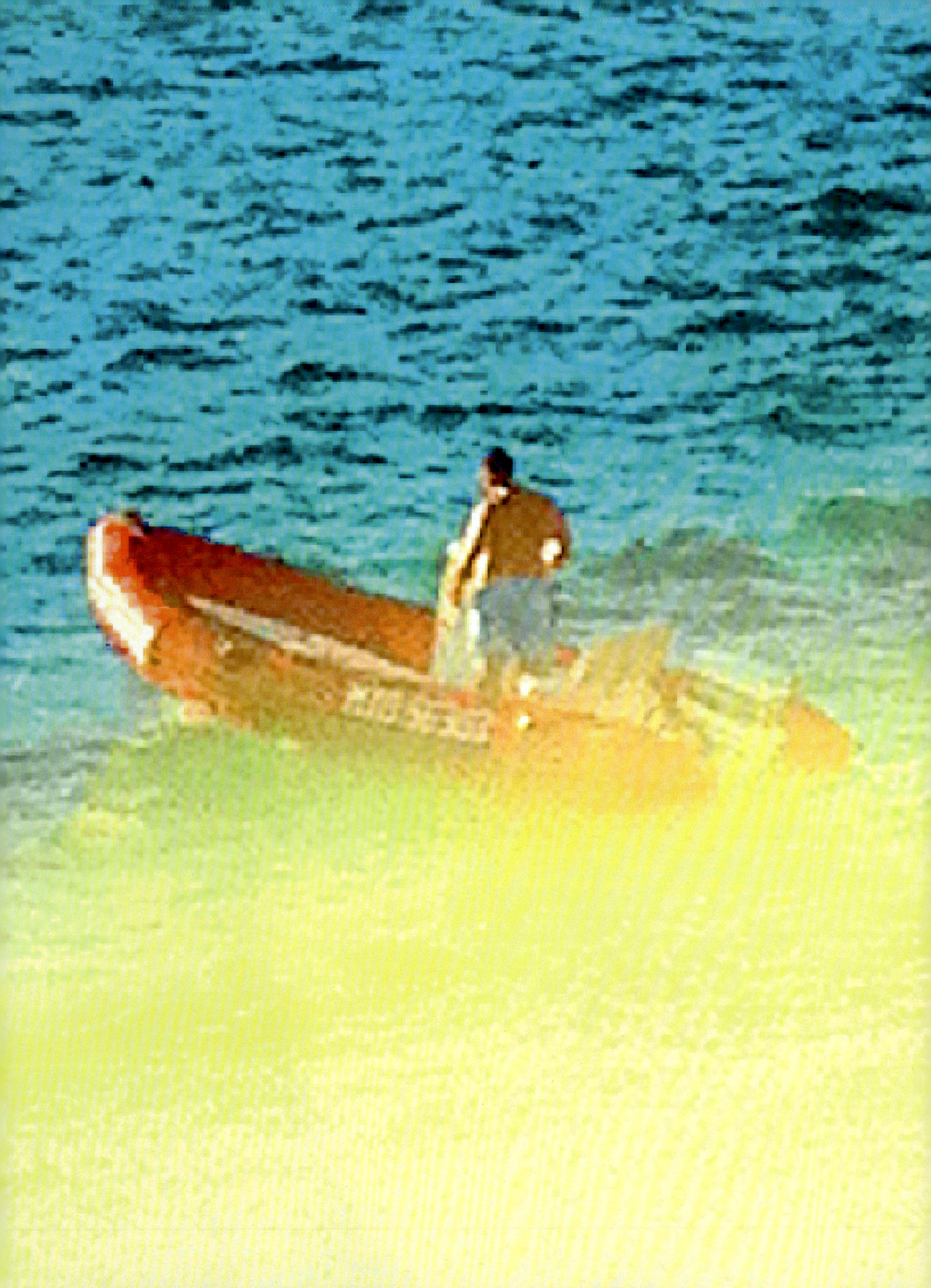

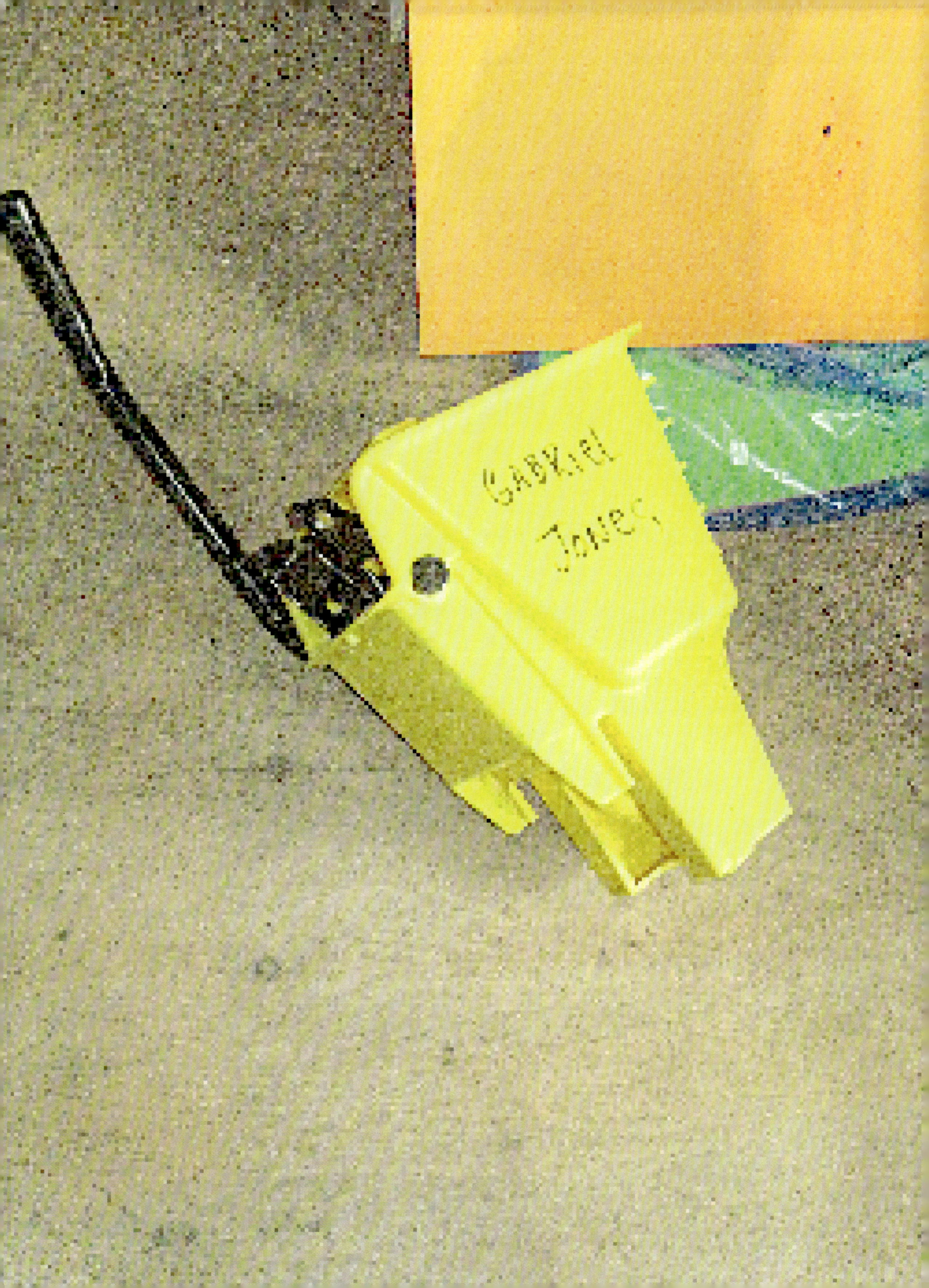
GABRIEL
JONES

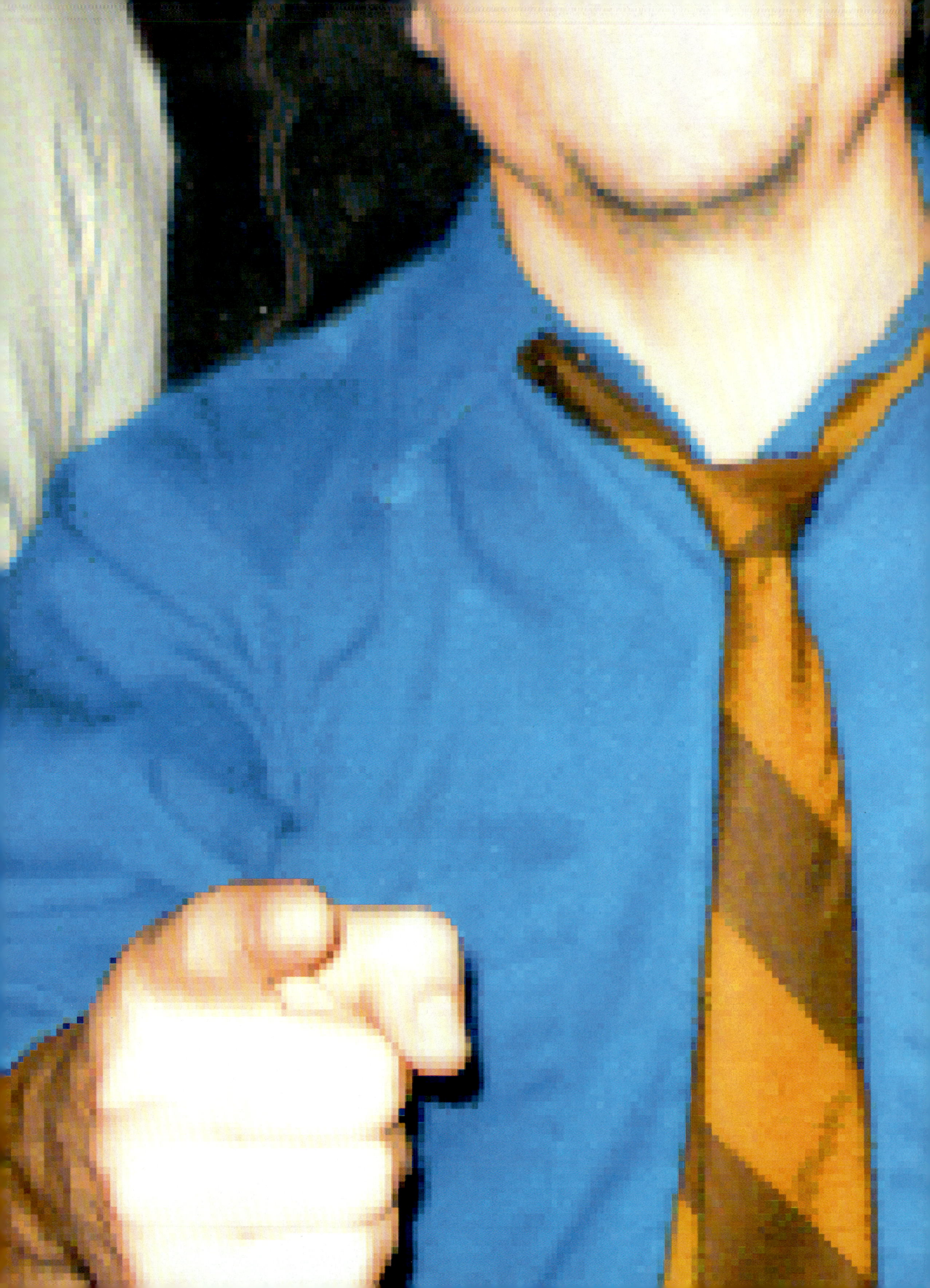

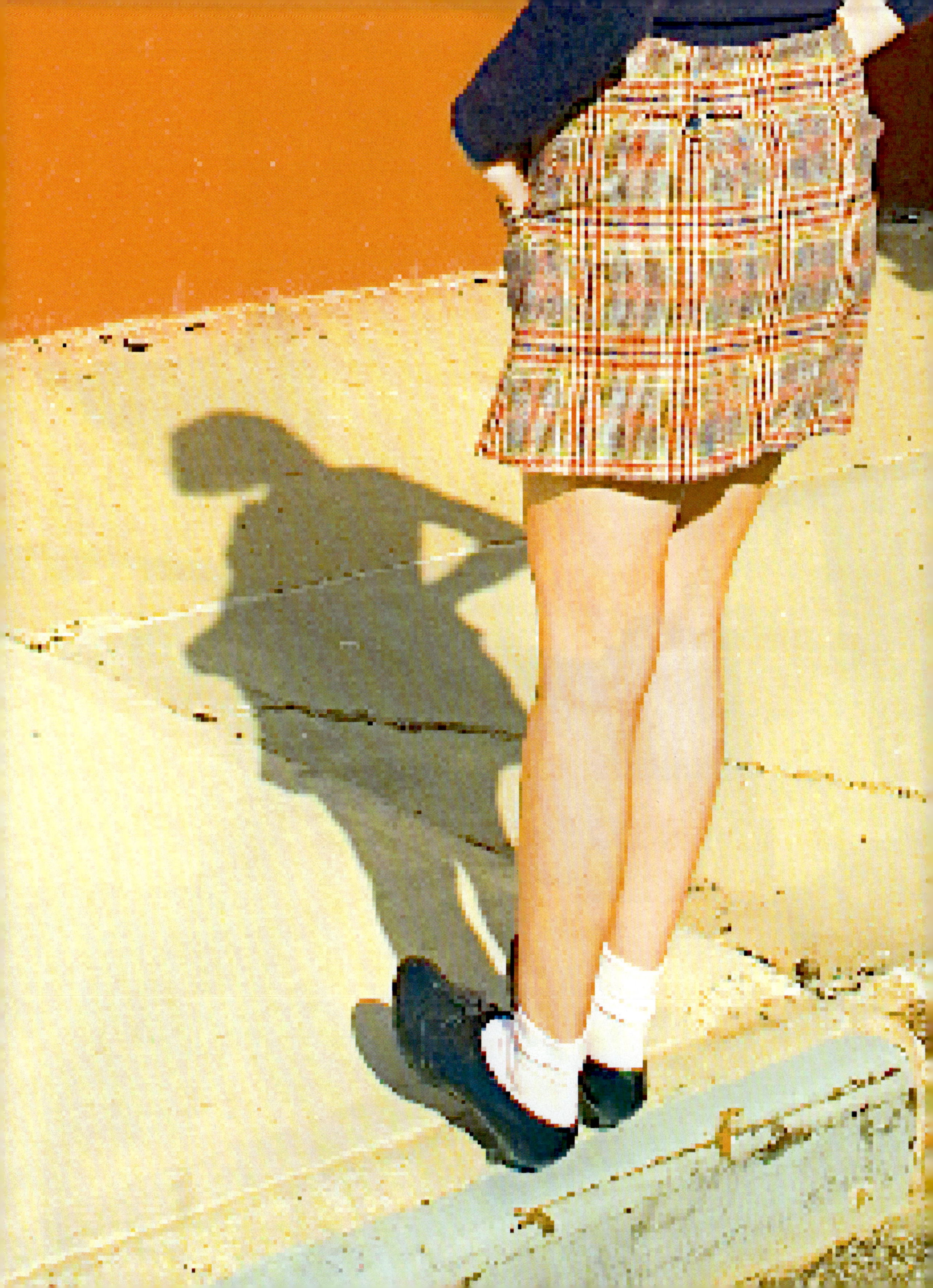

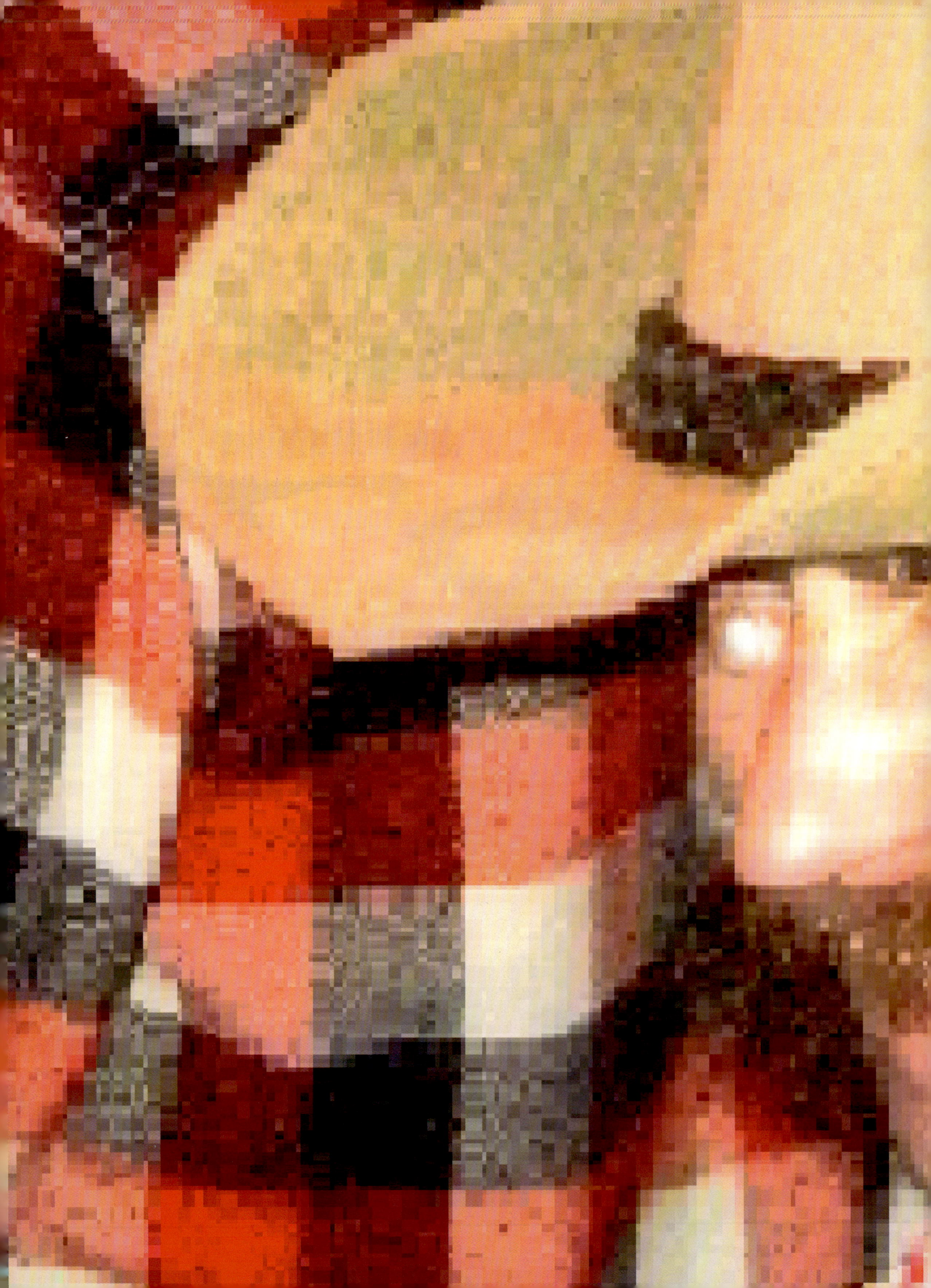

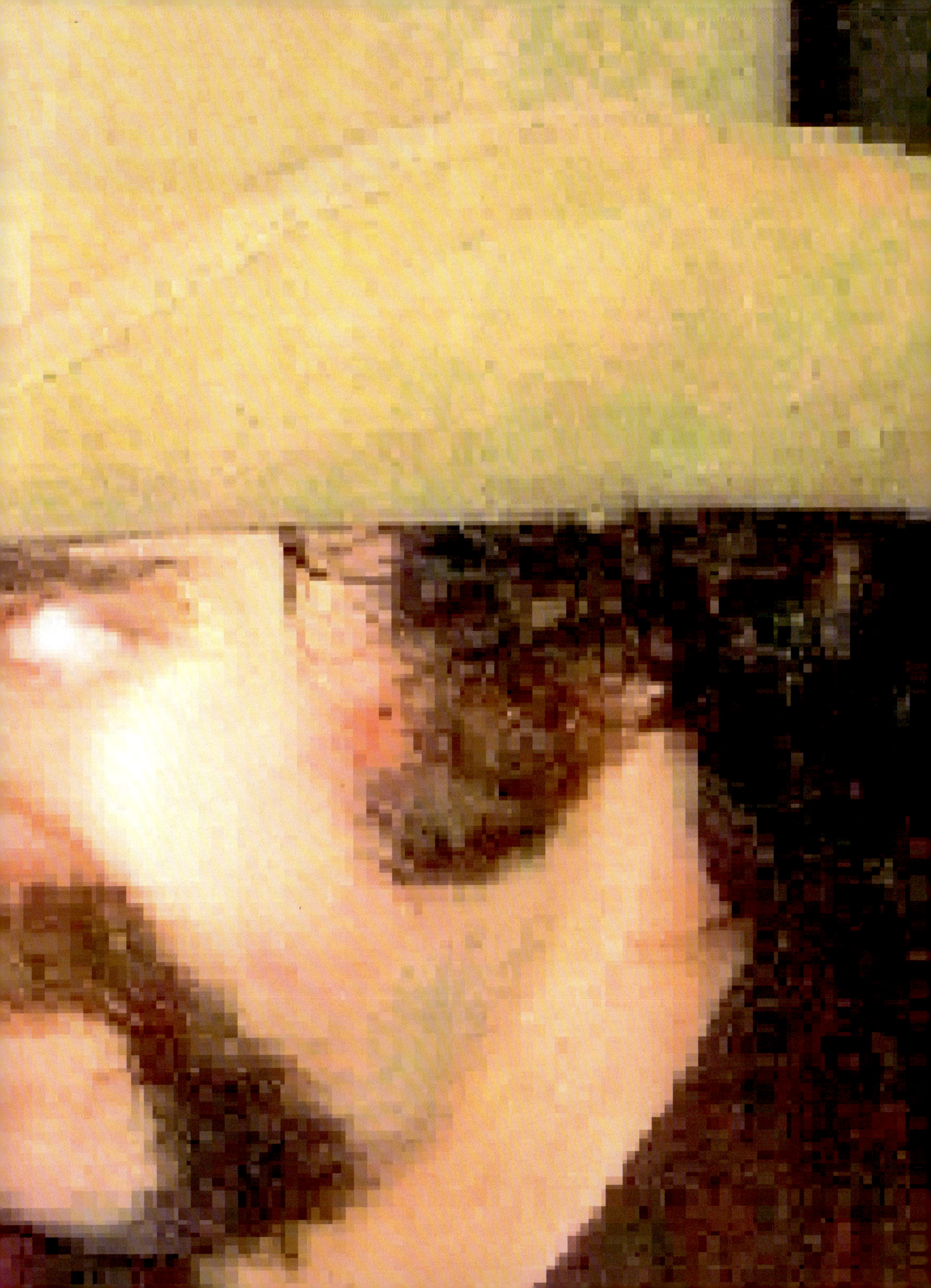

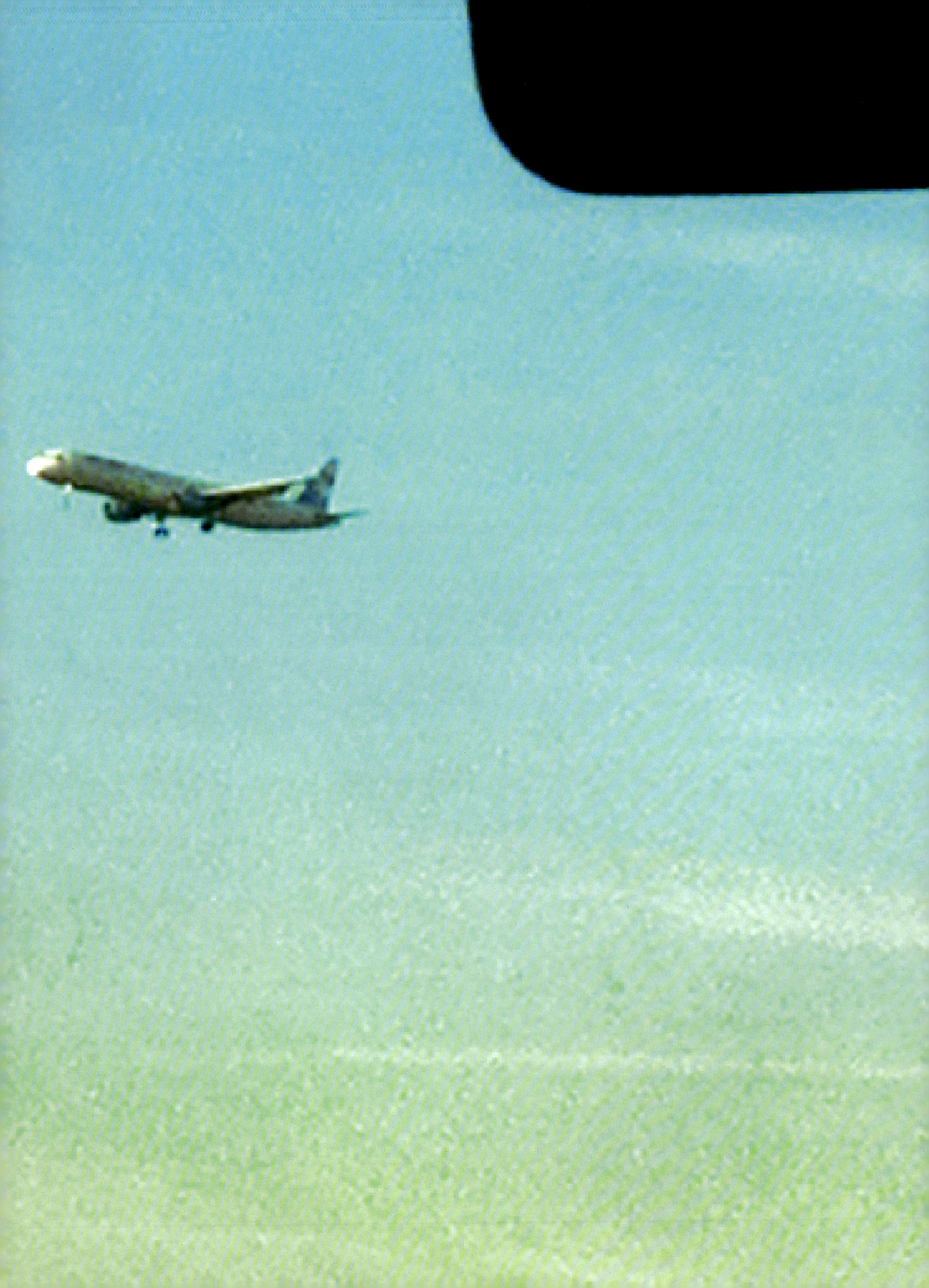

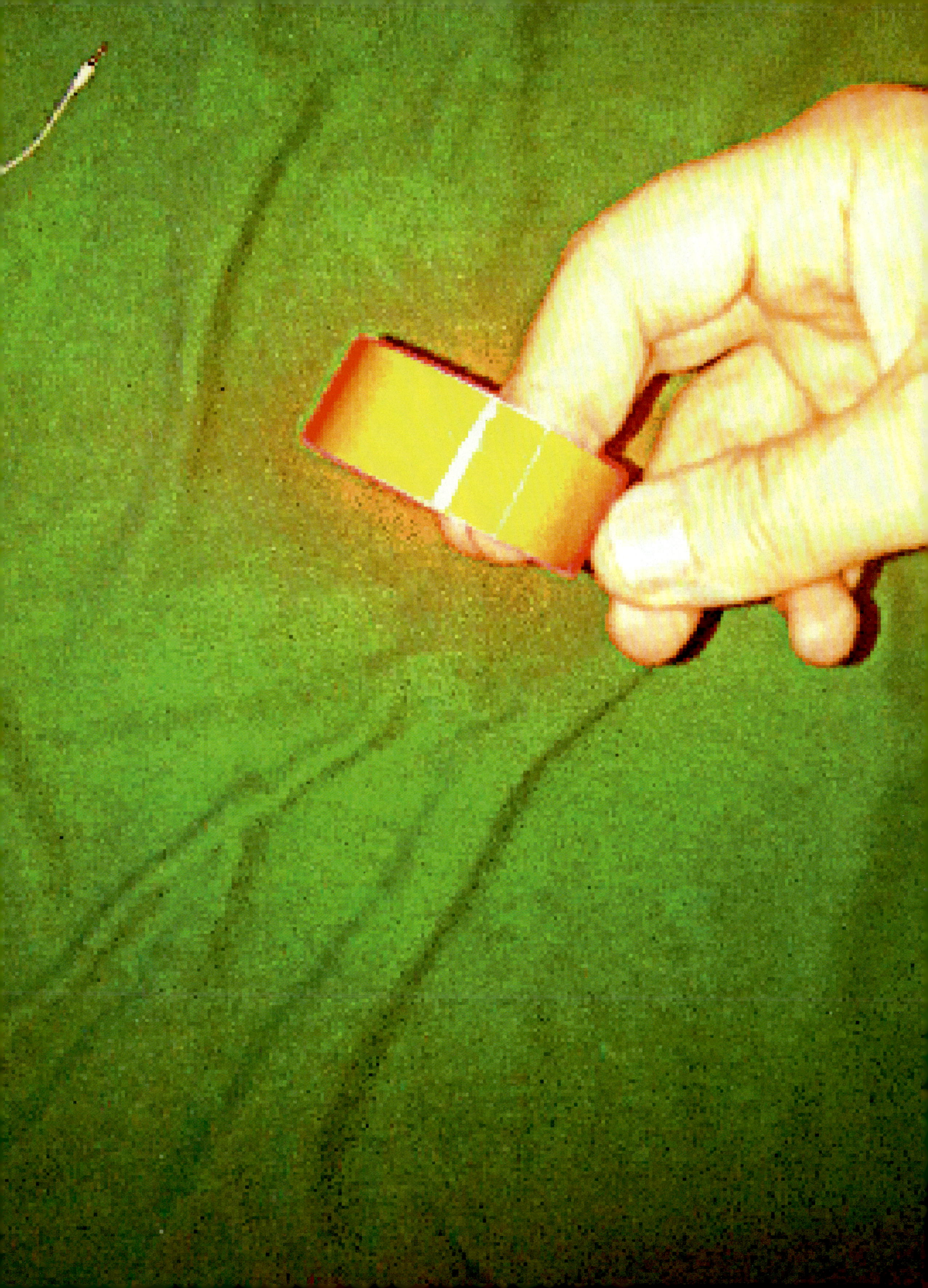

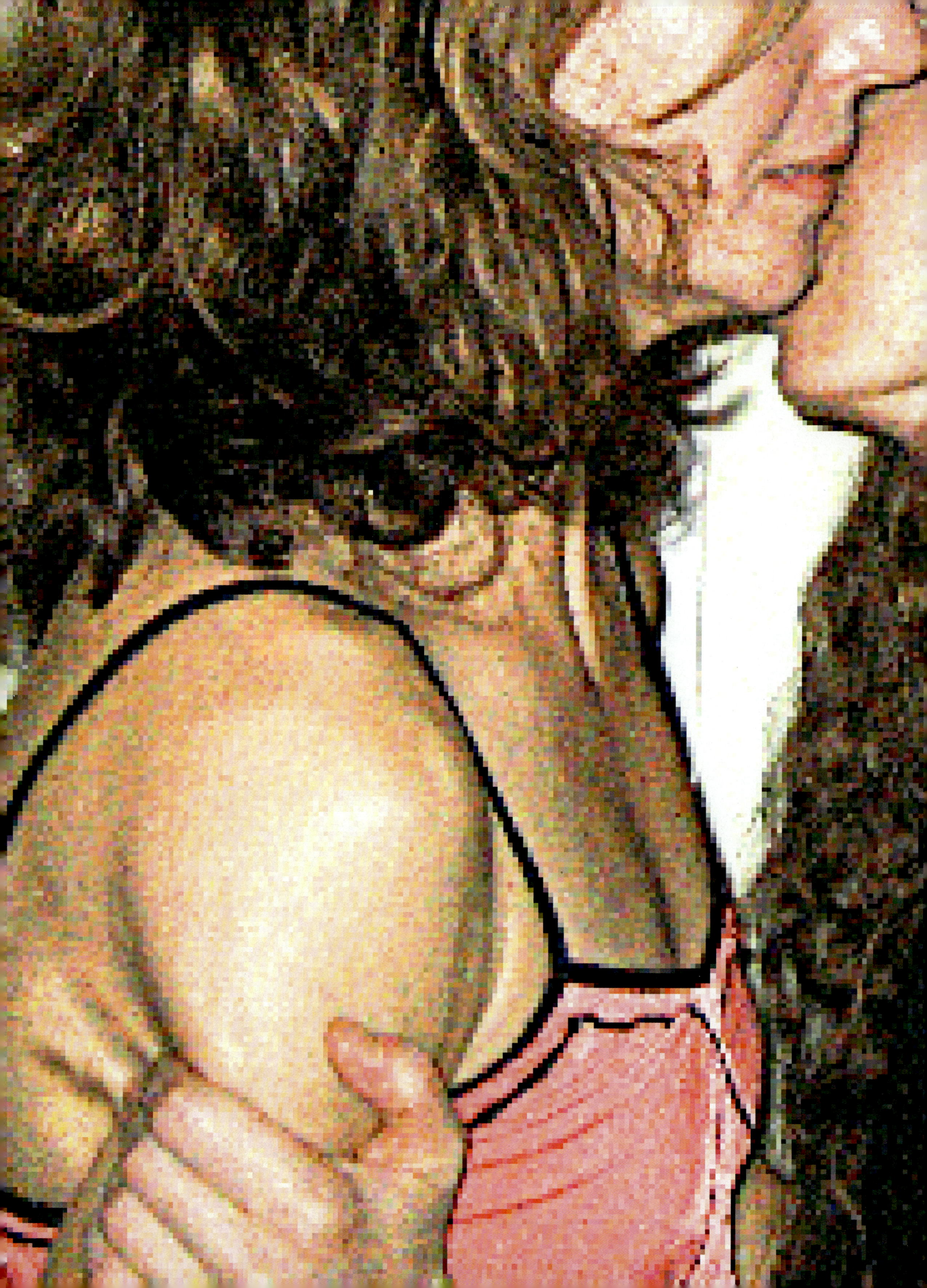

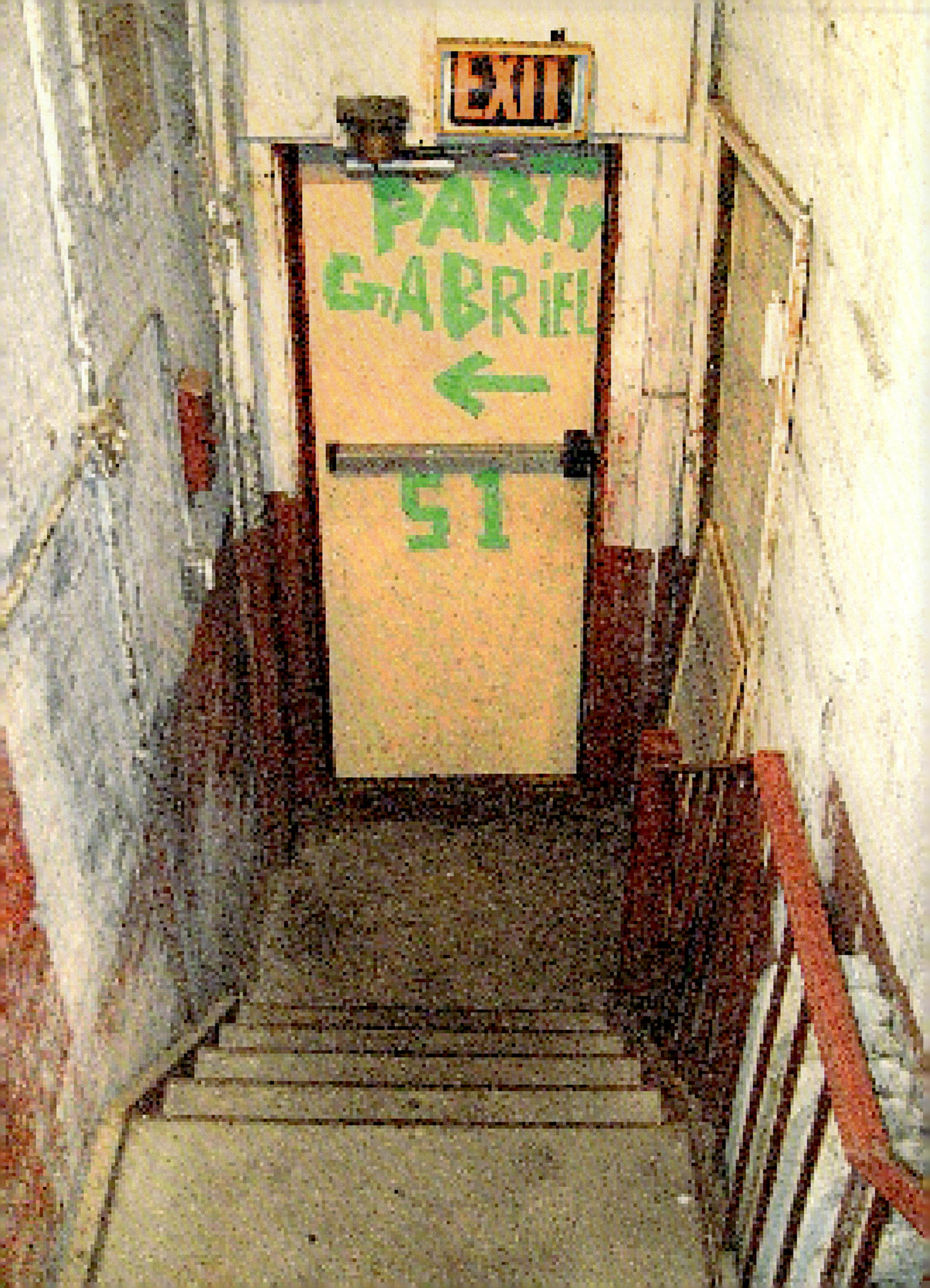

EXIT
GABRIEL
51

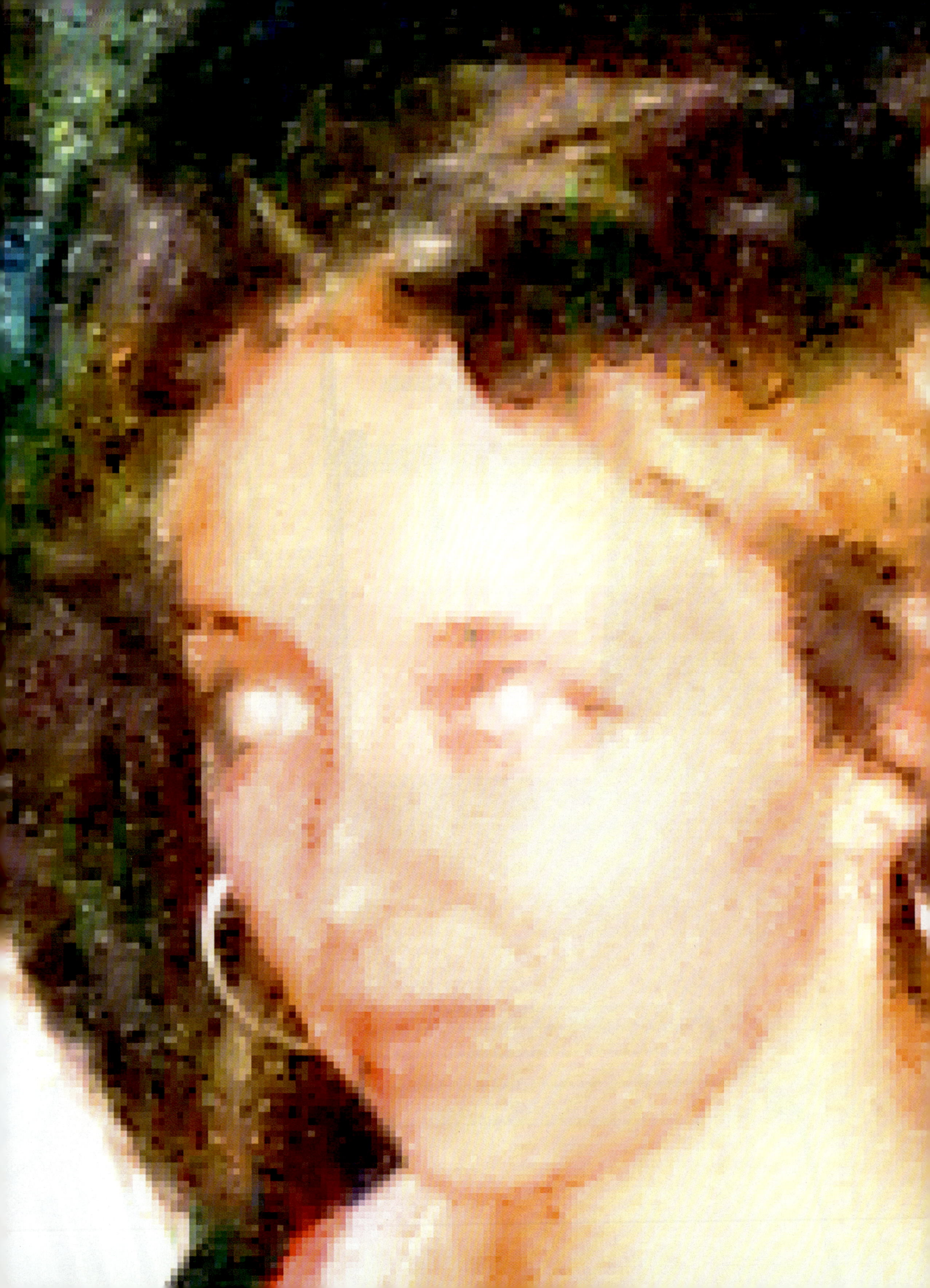

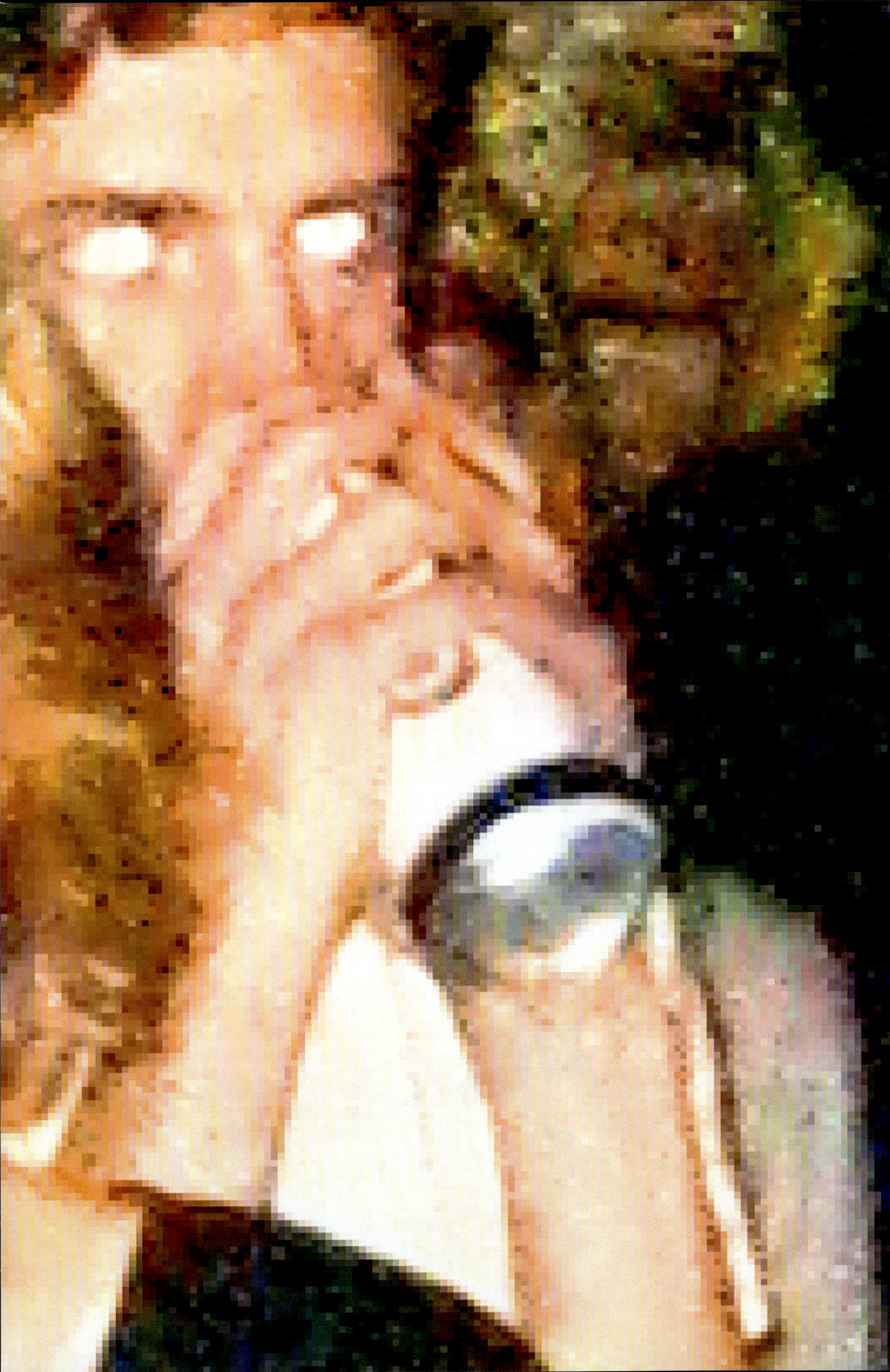

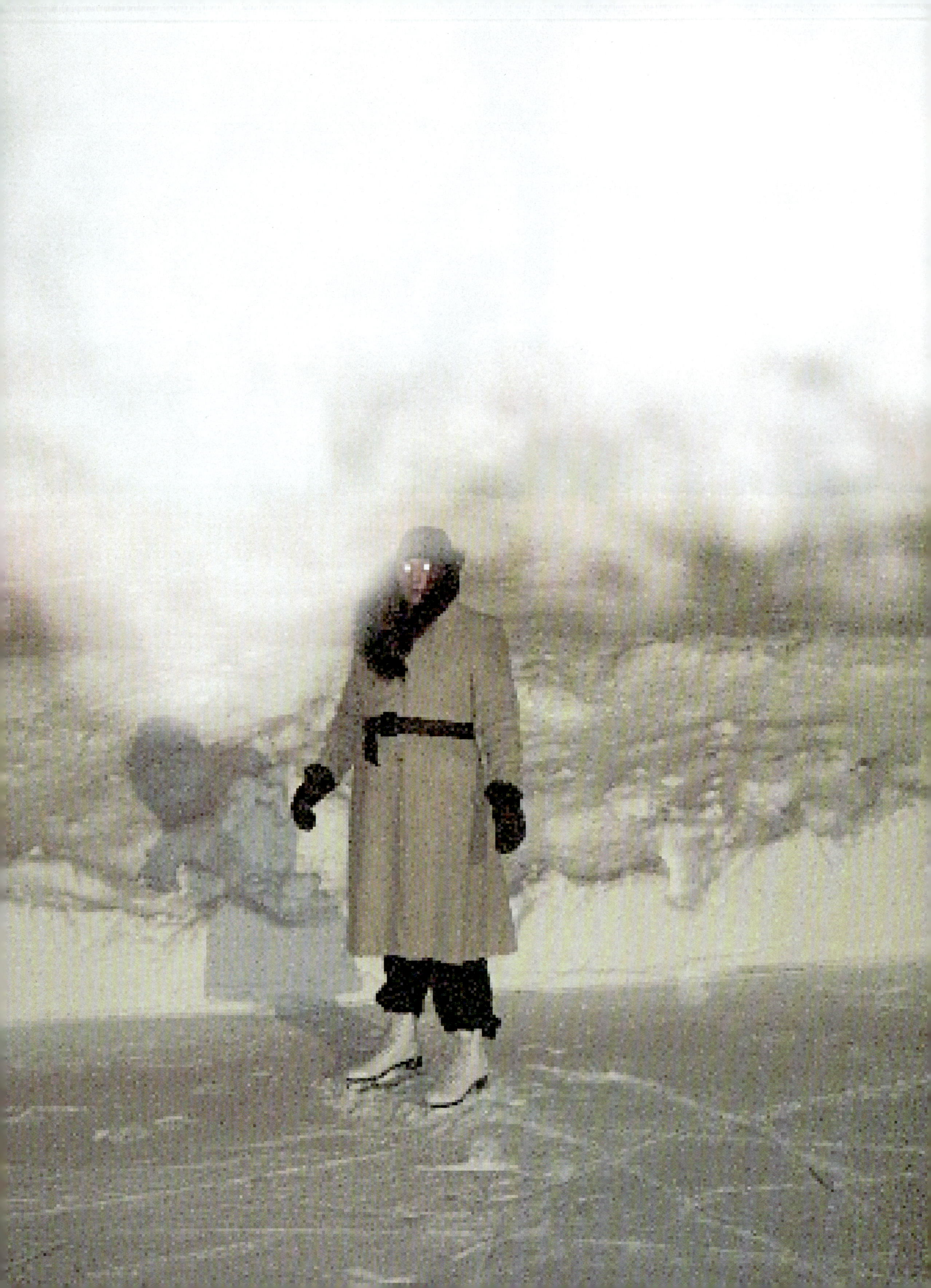

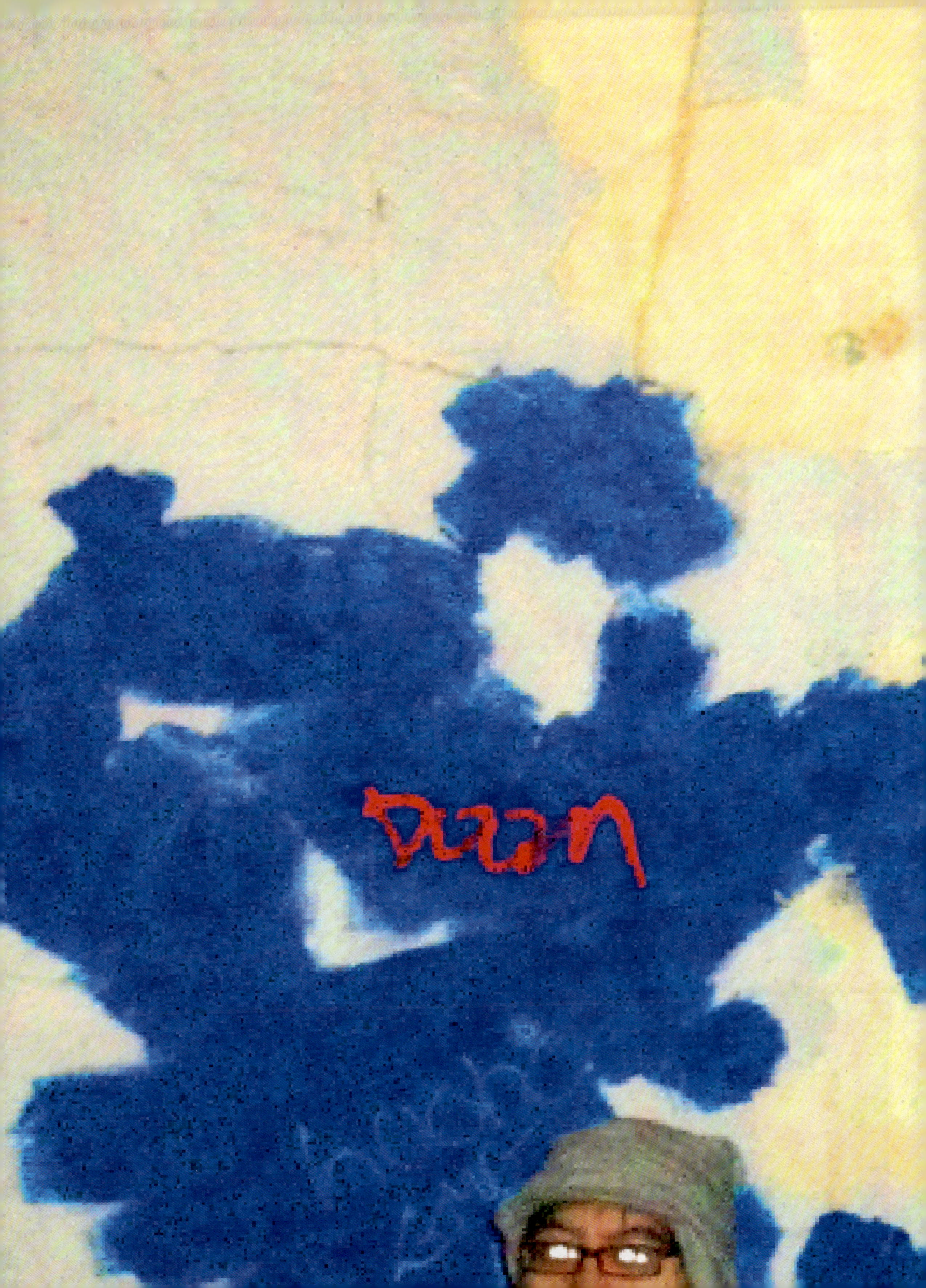

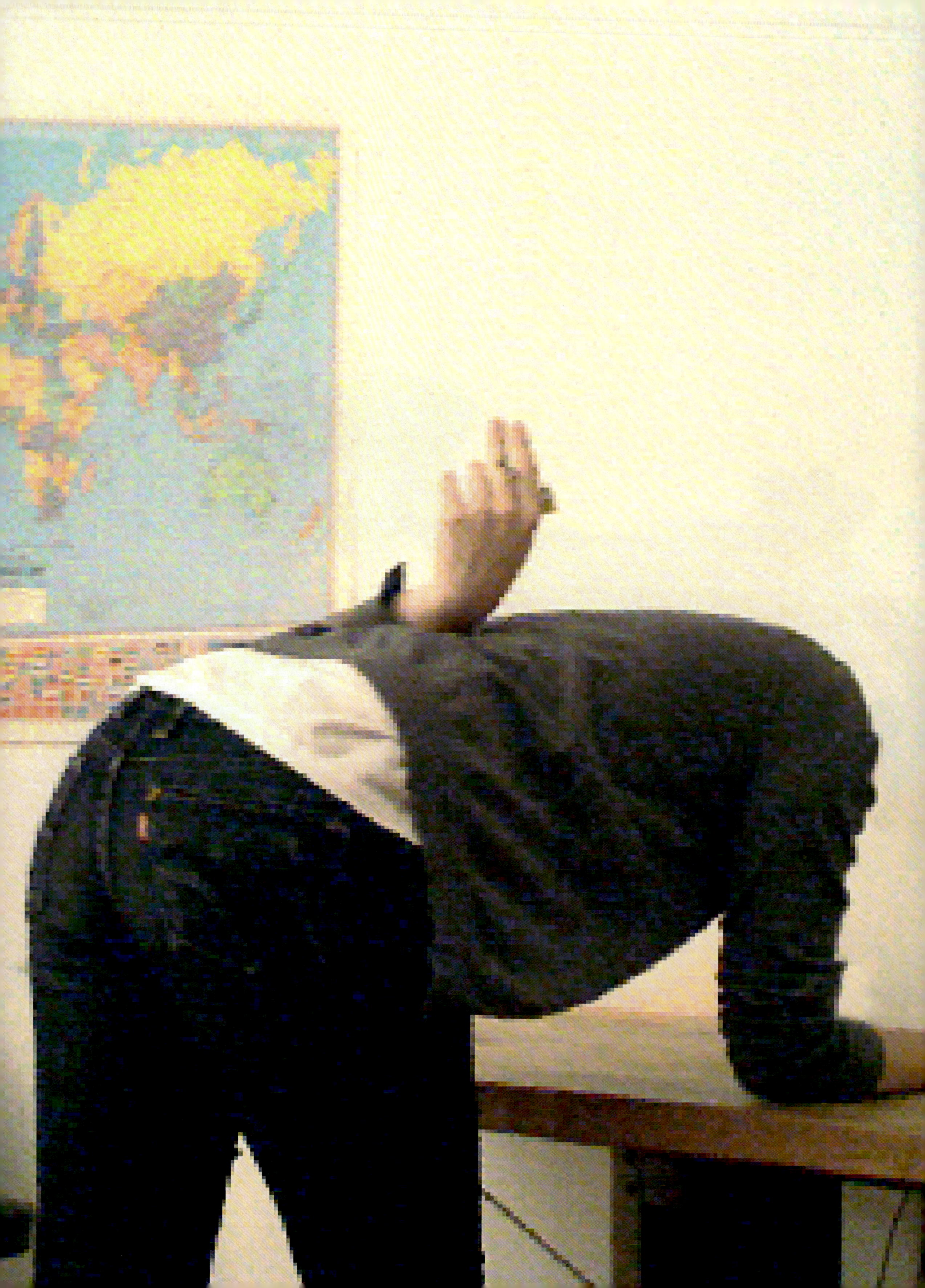

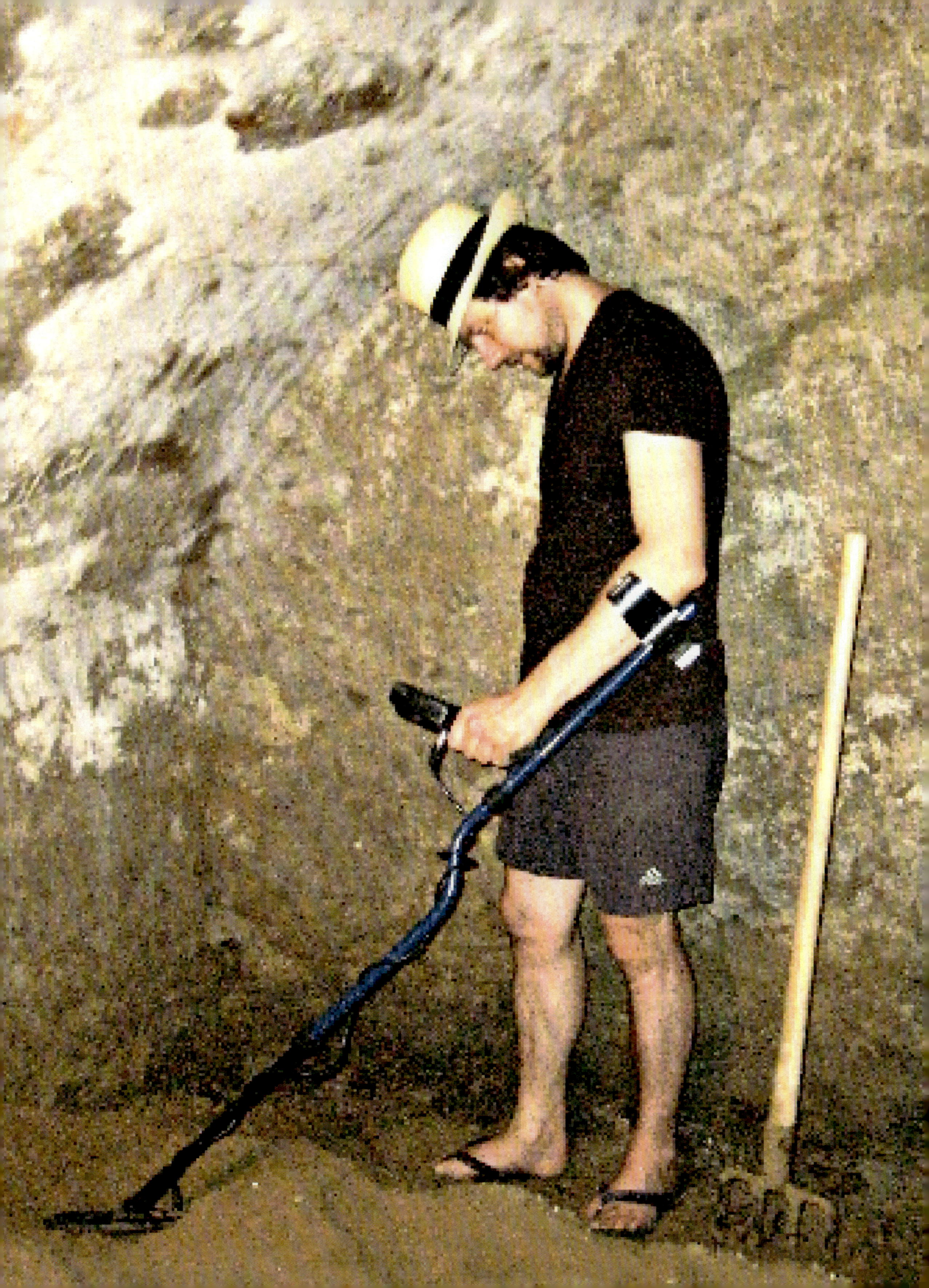

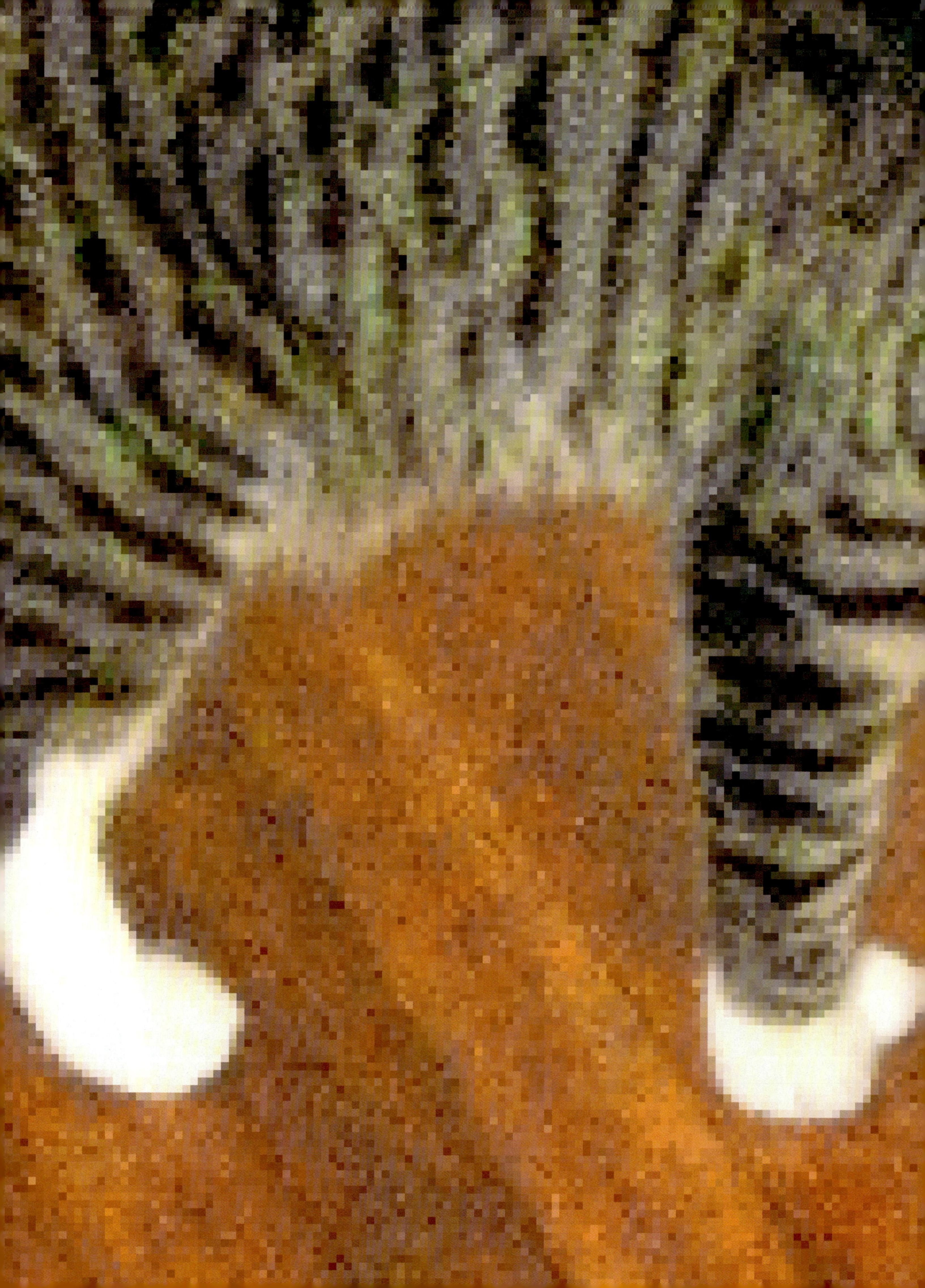

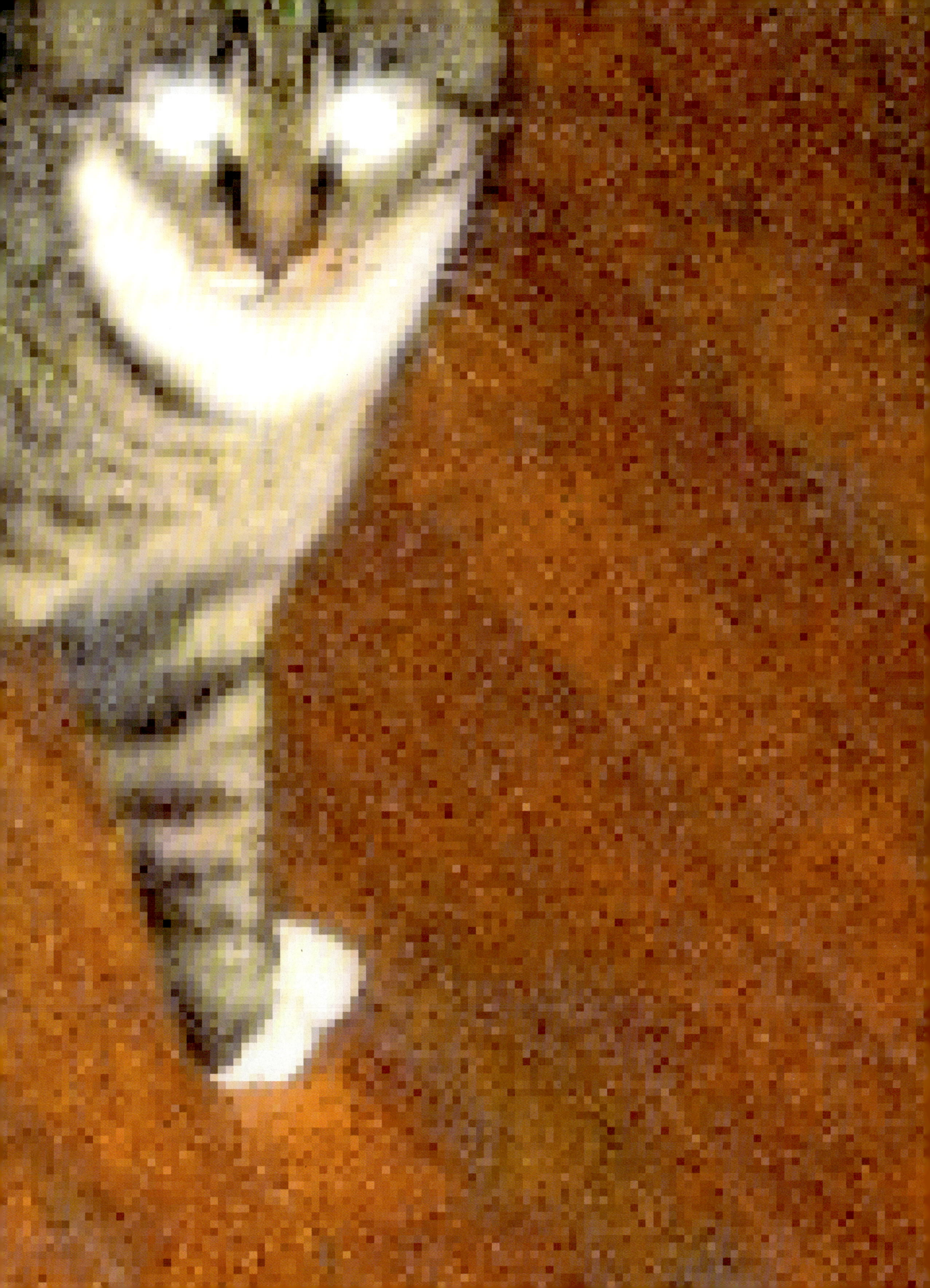

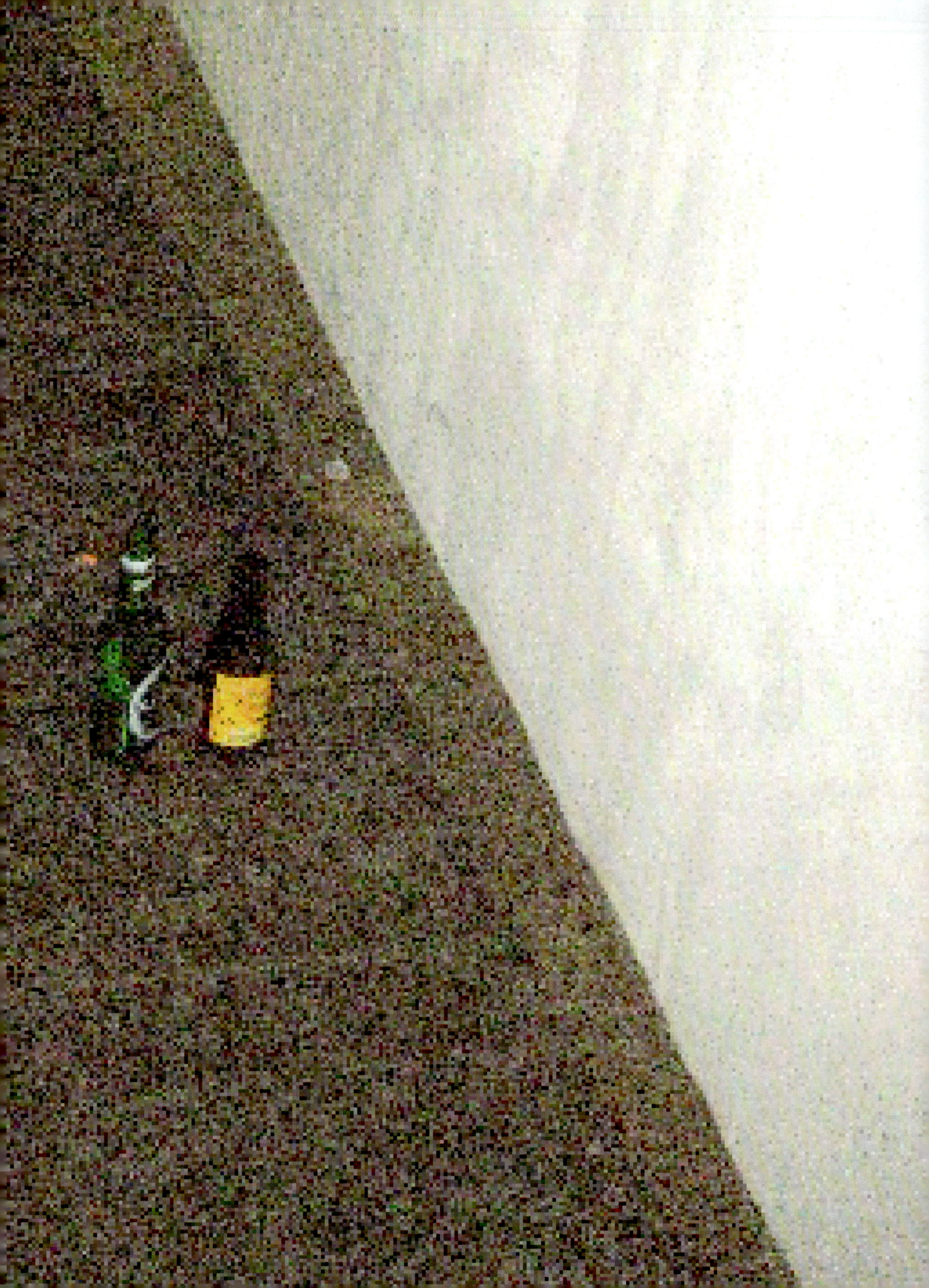

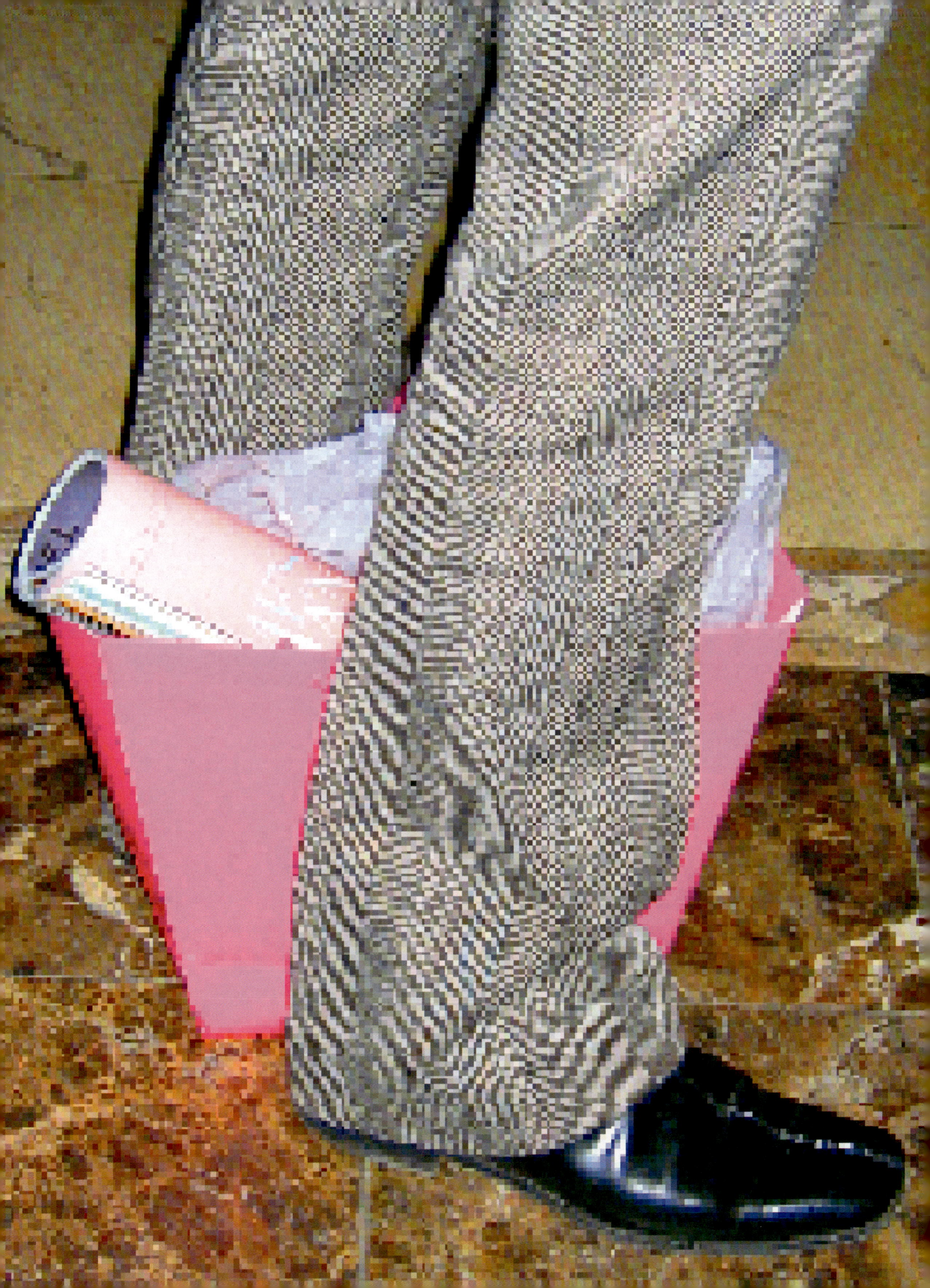

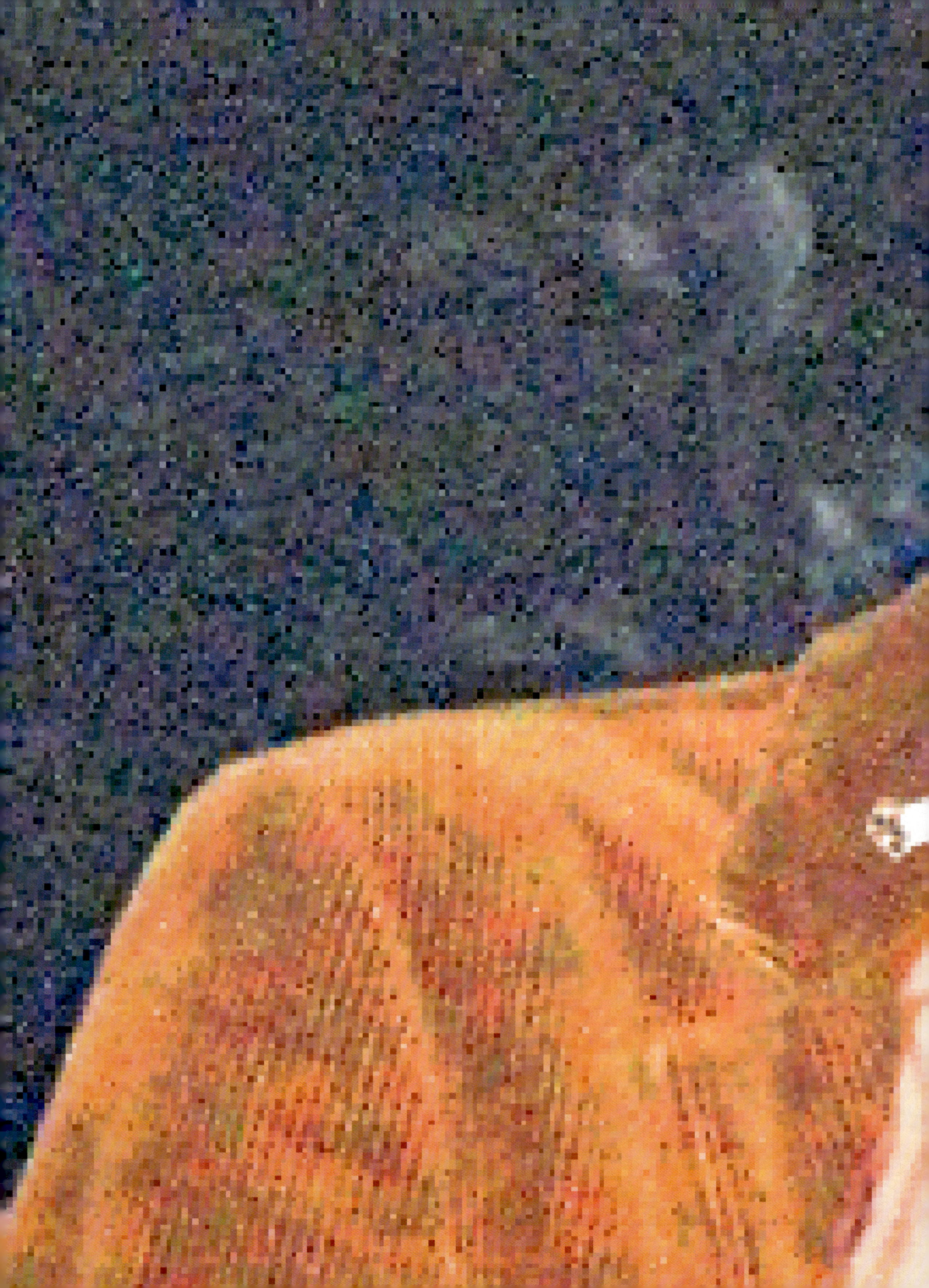

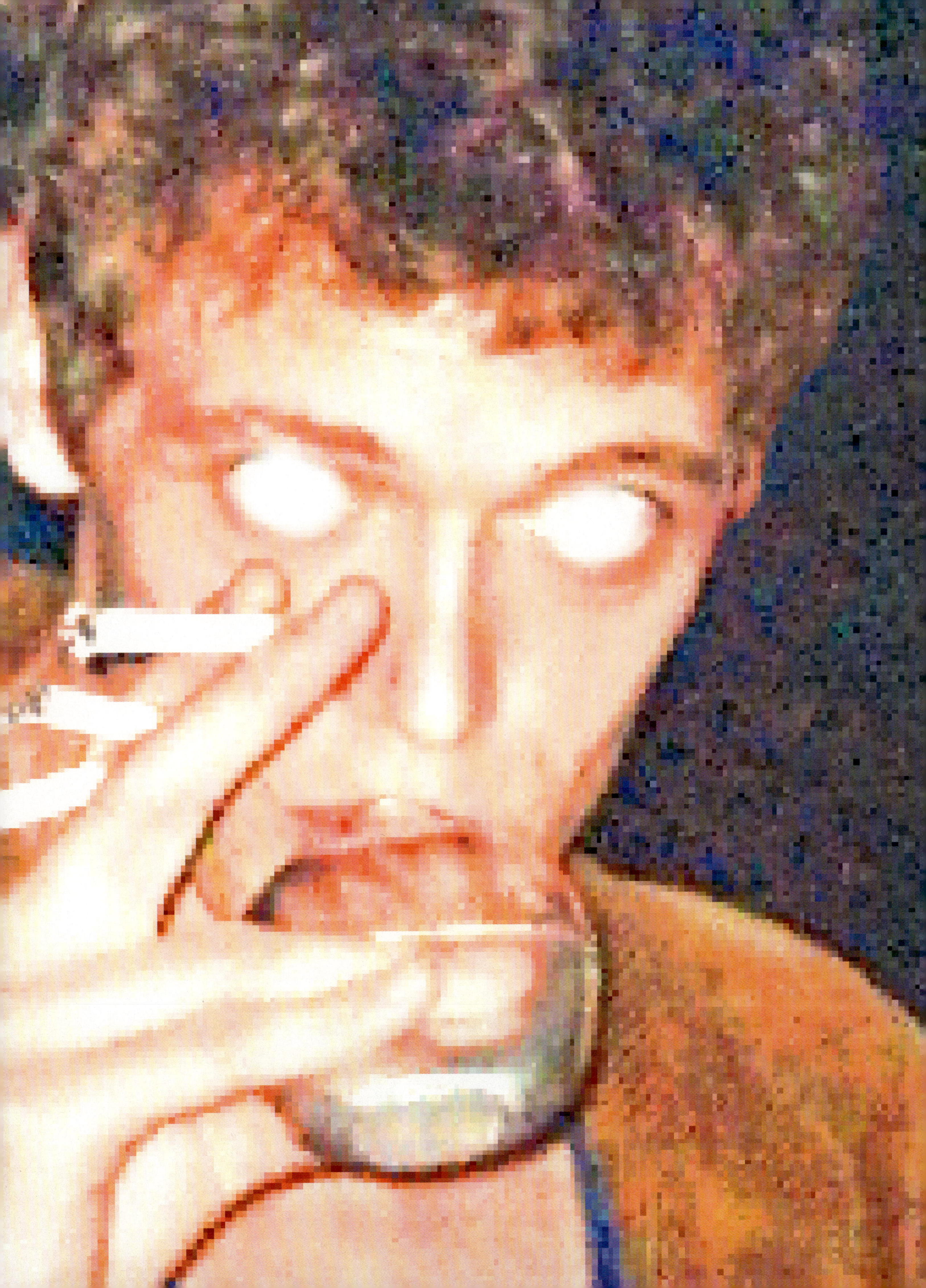

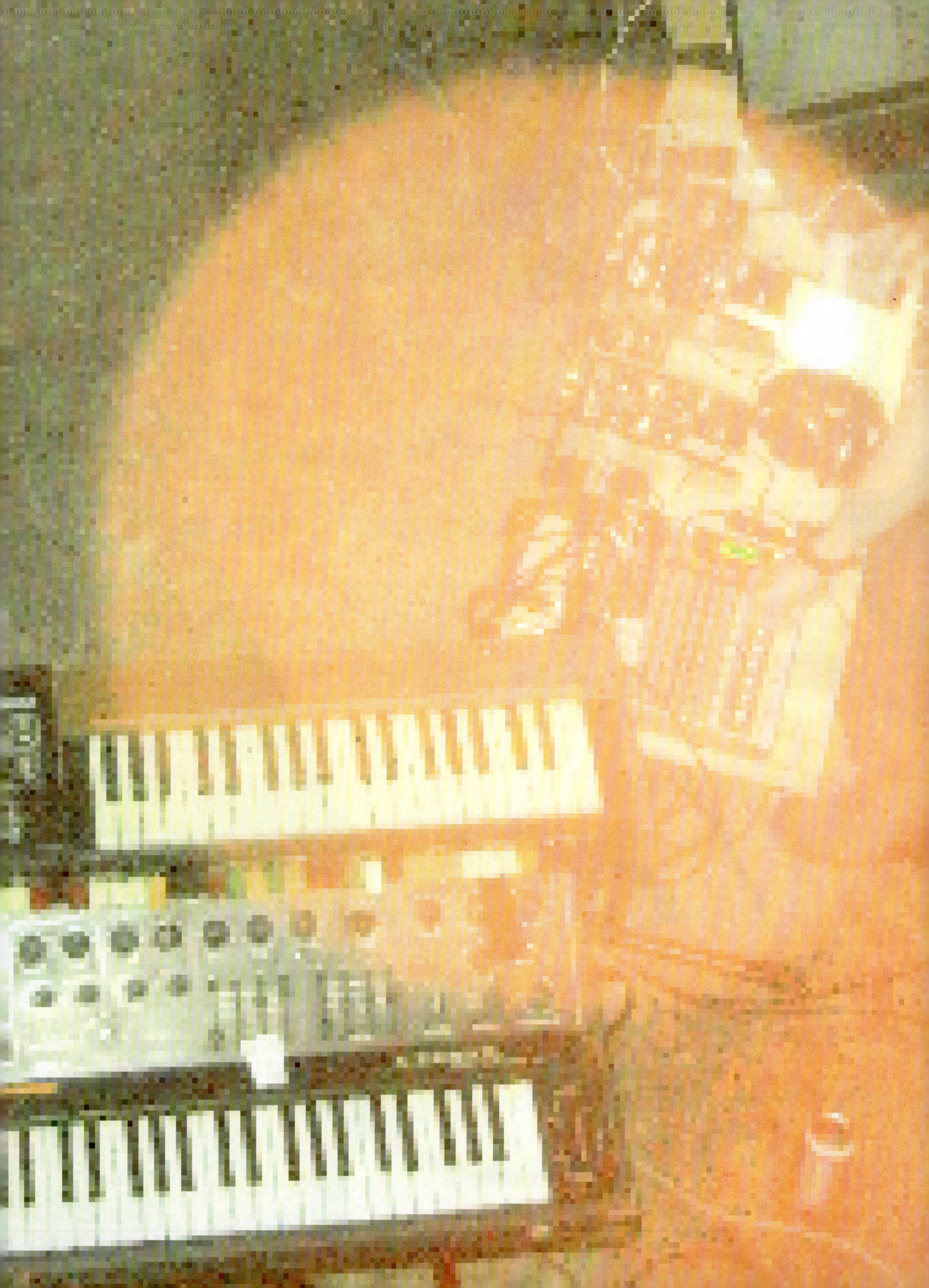

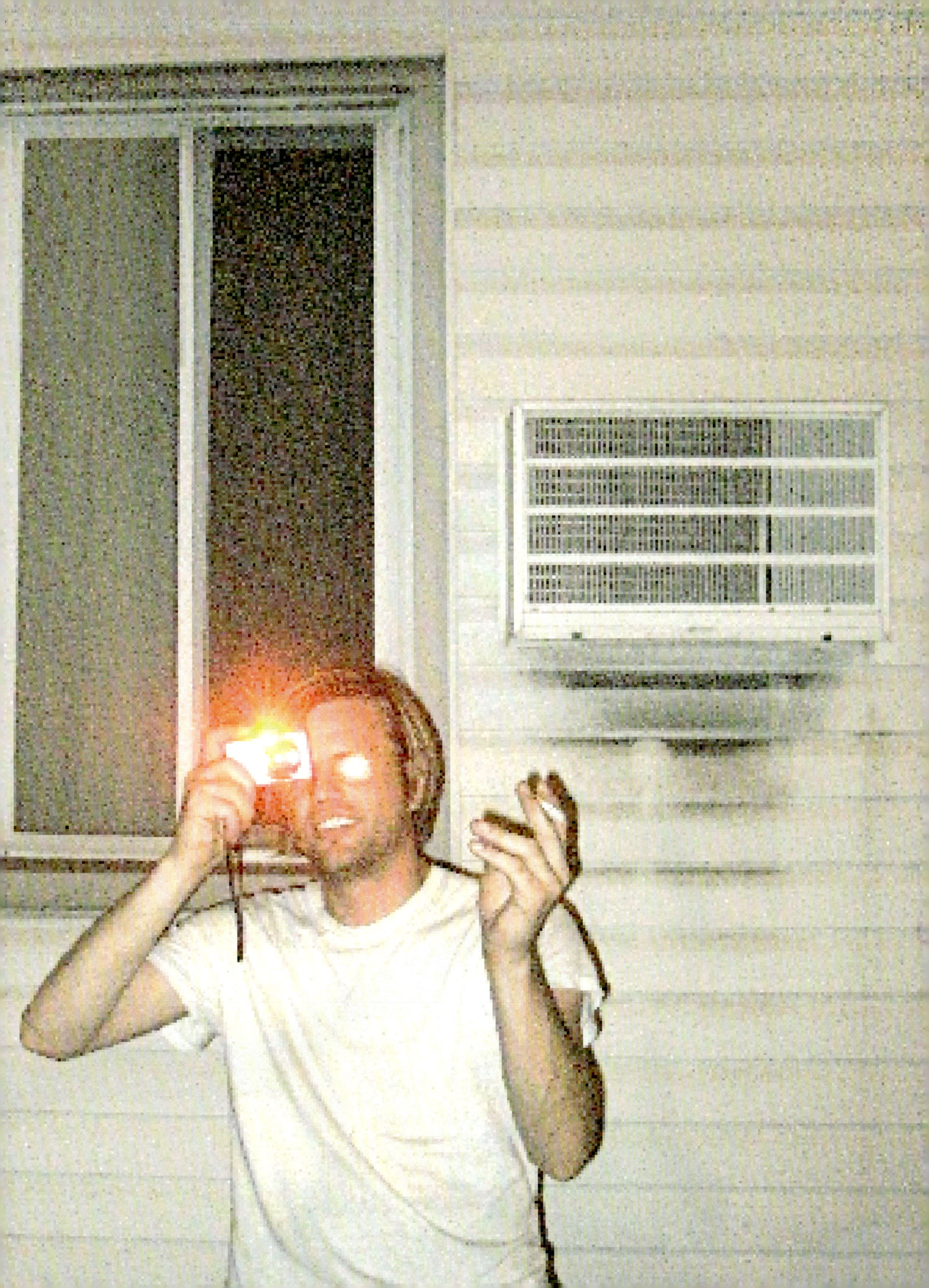

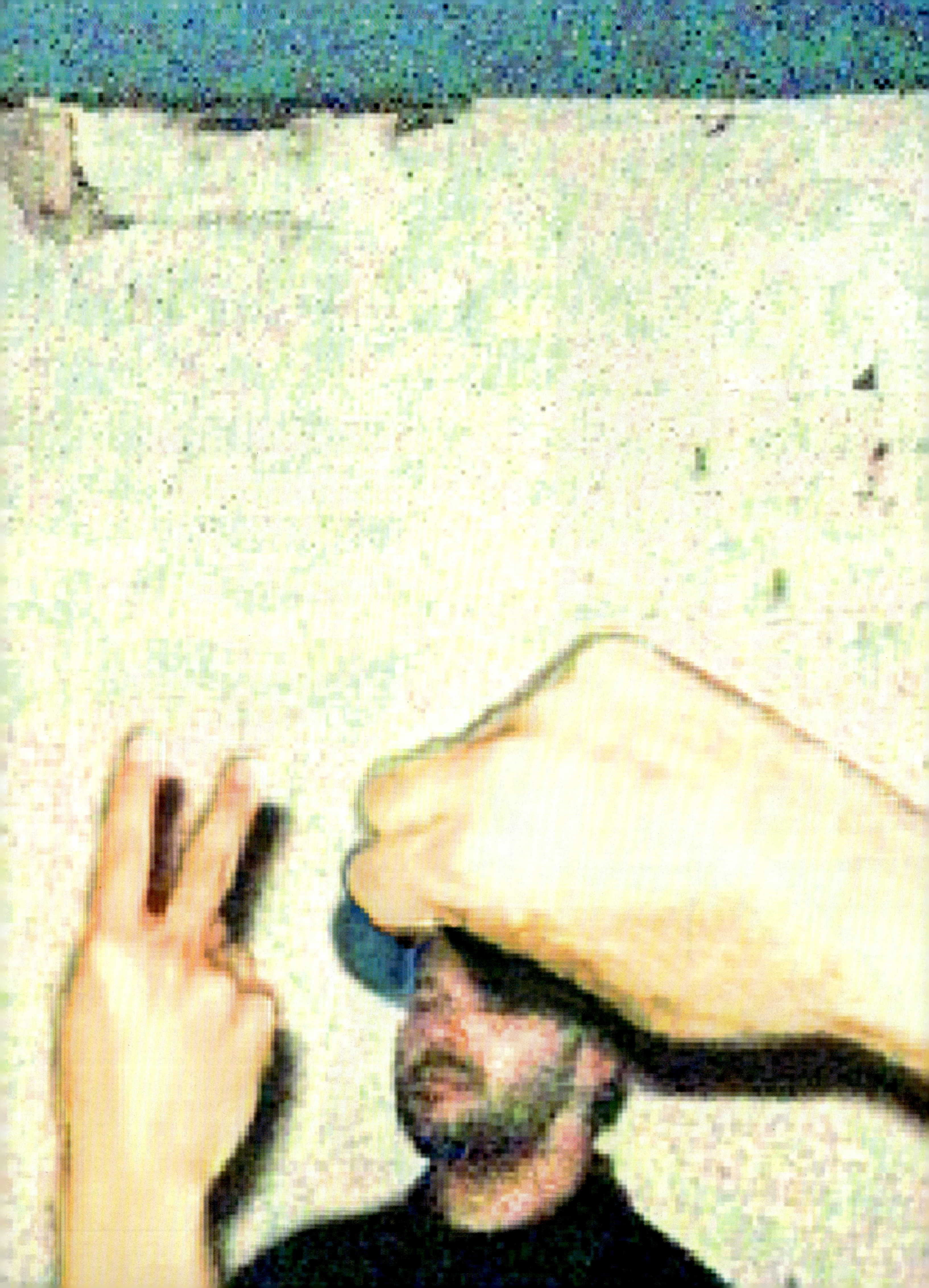

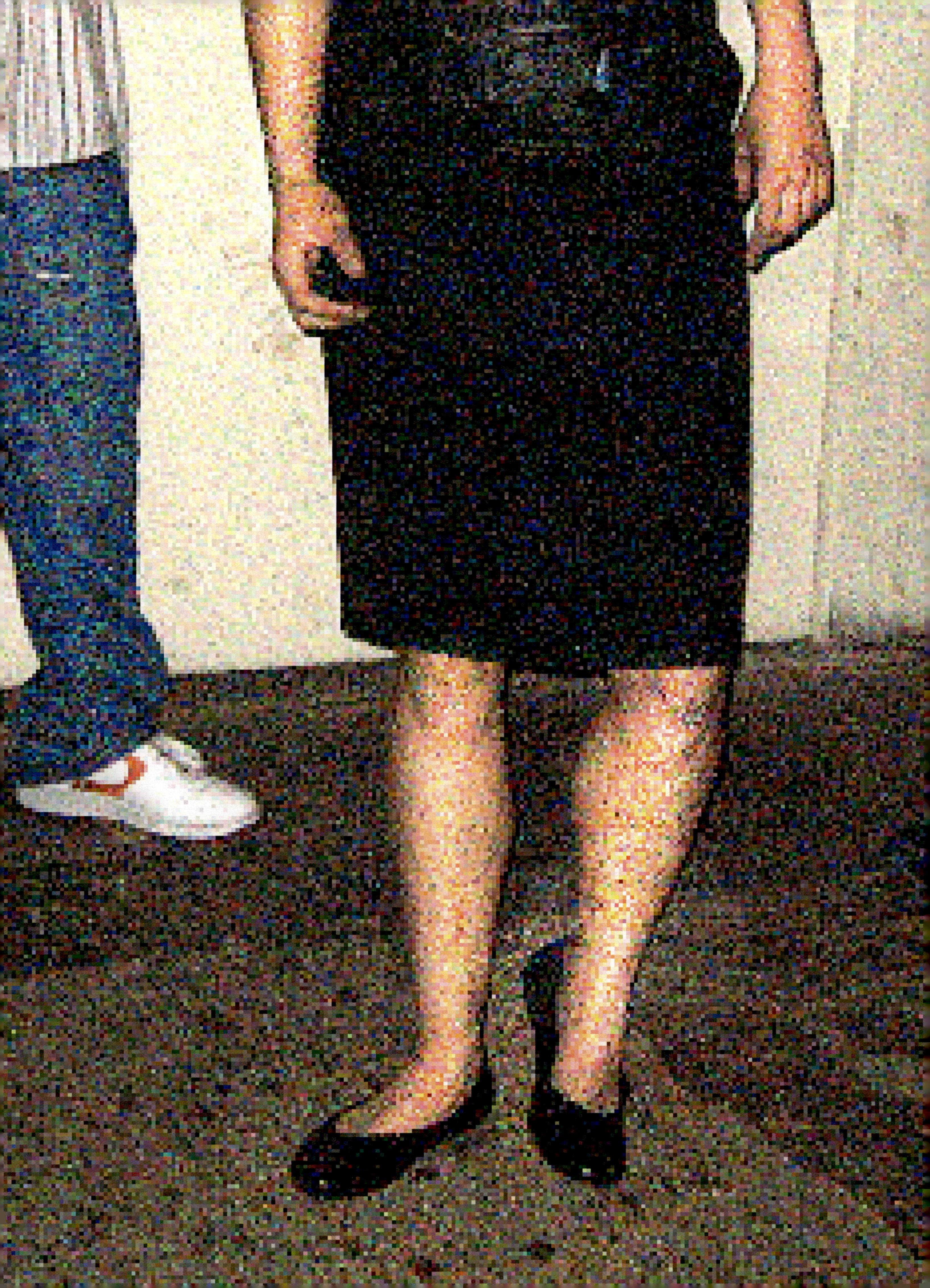

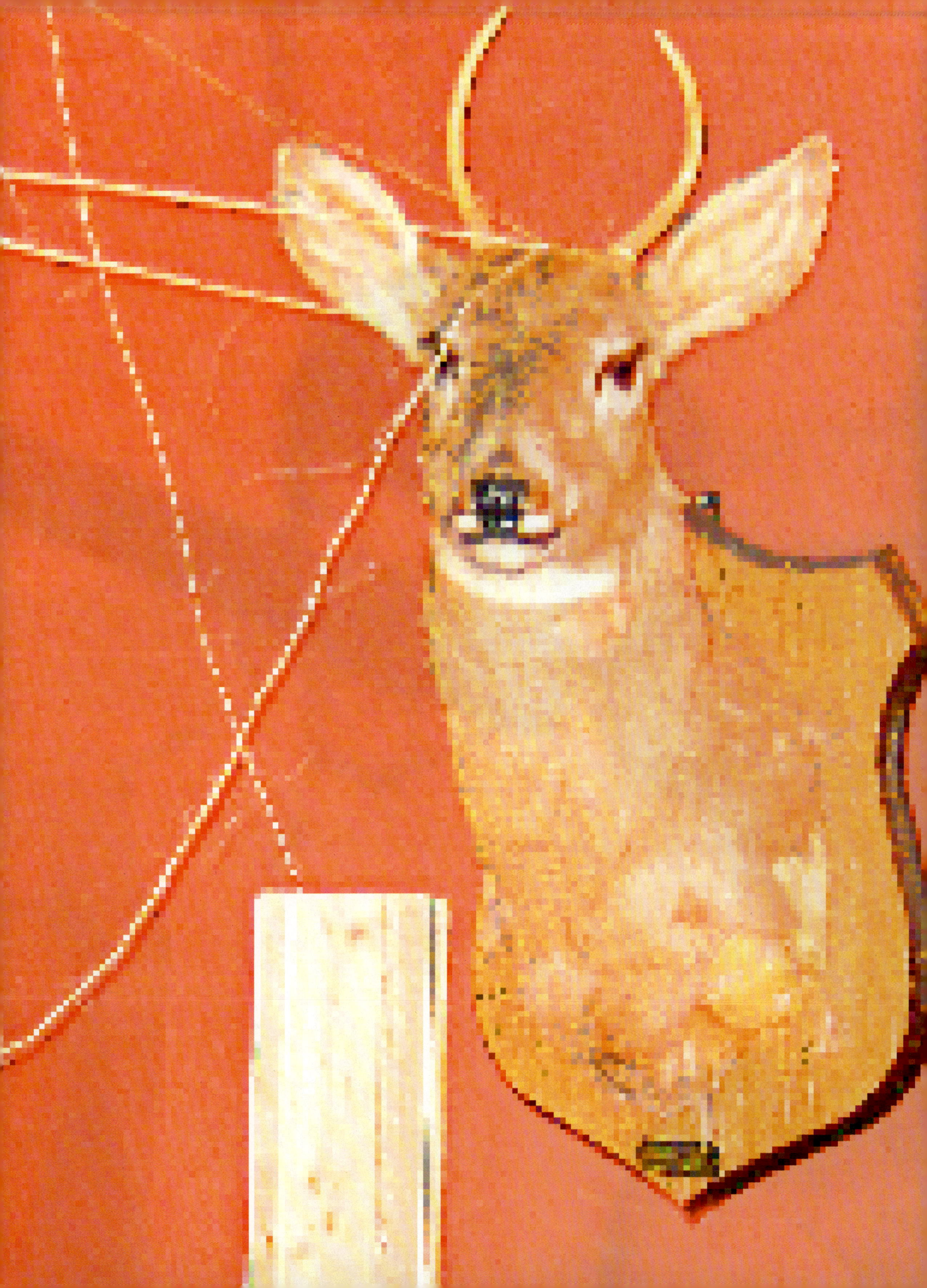

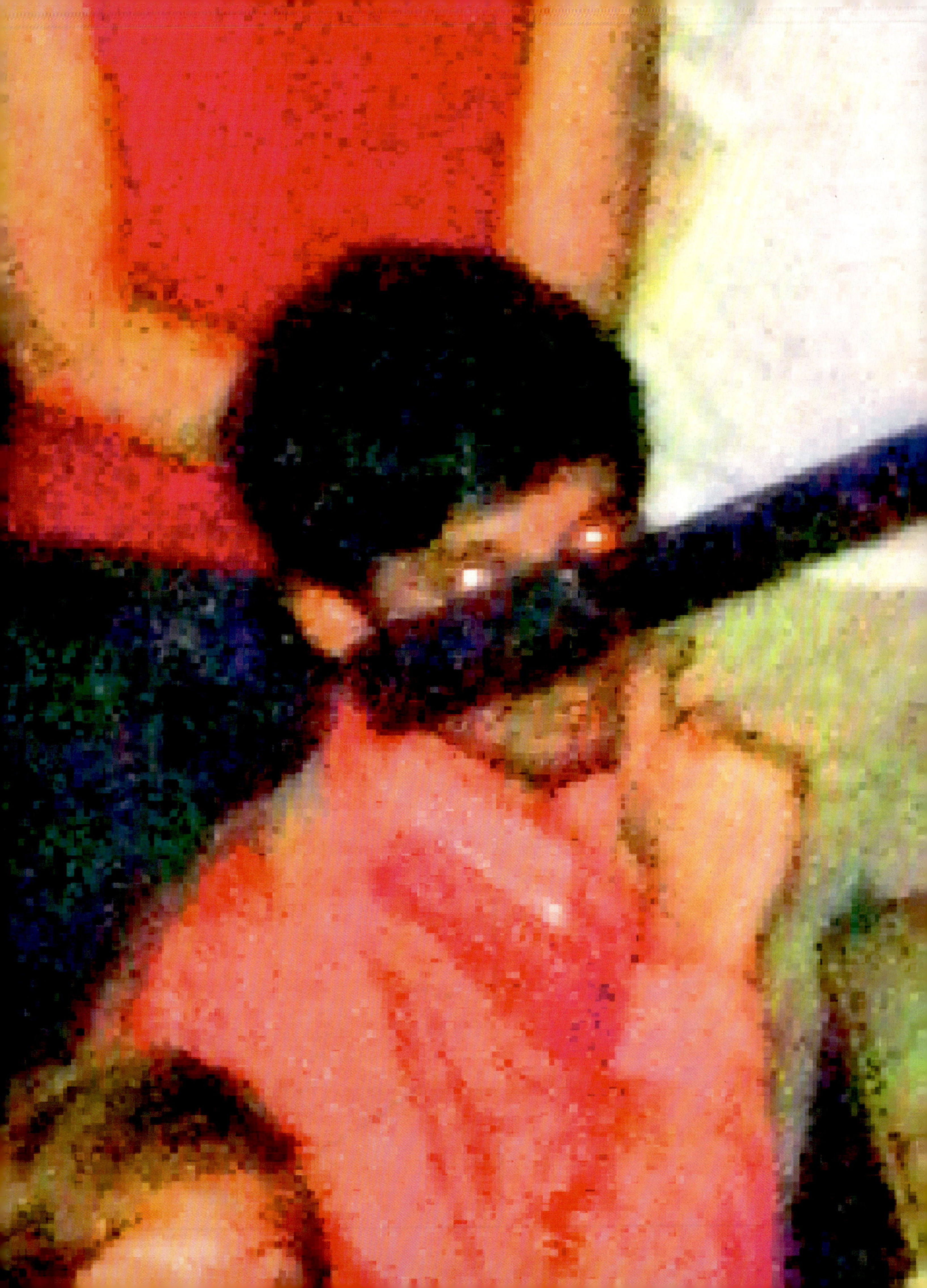

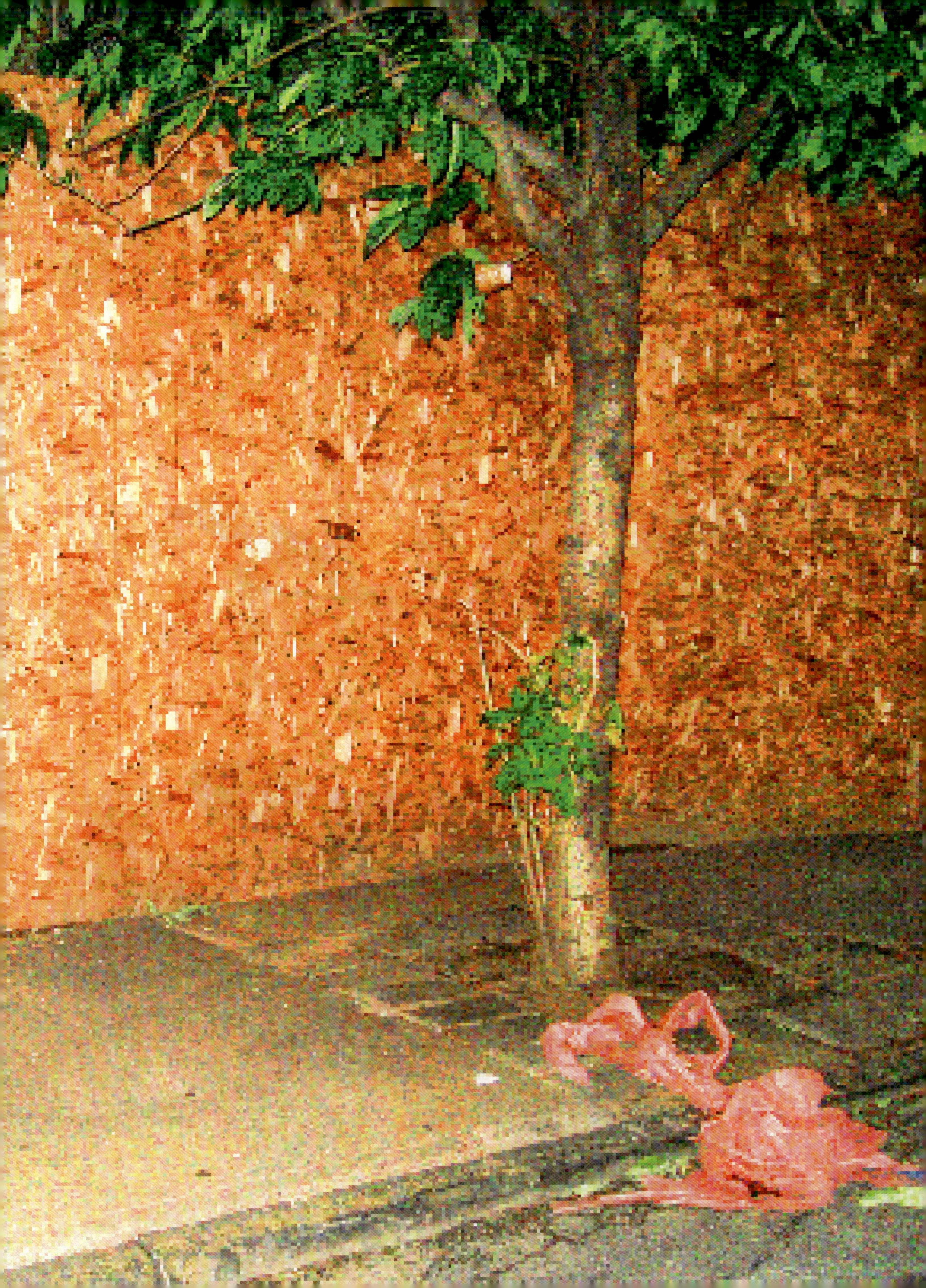

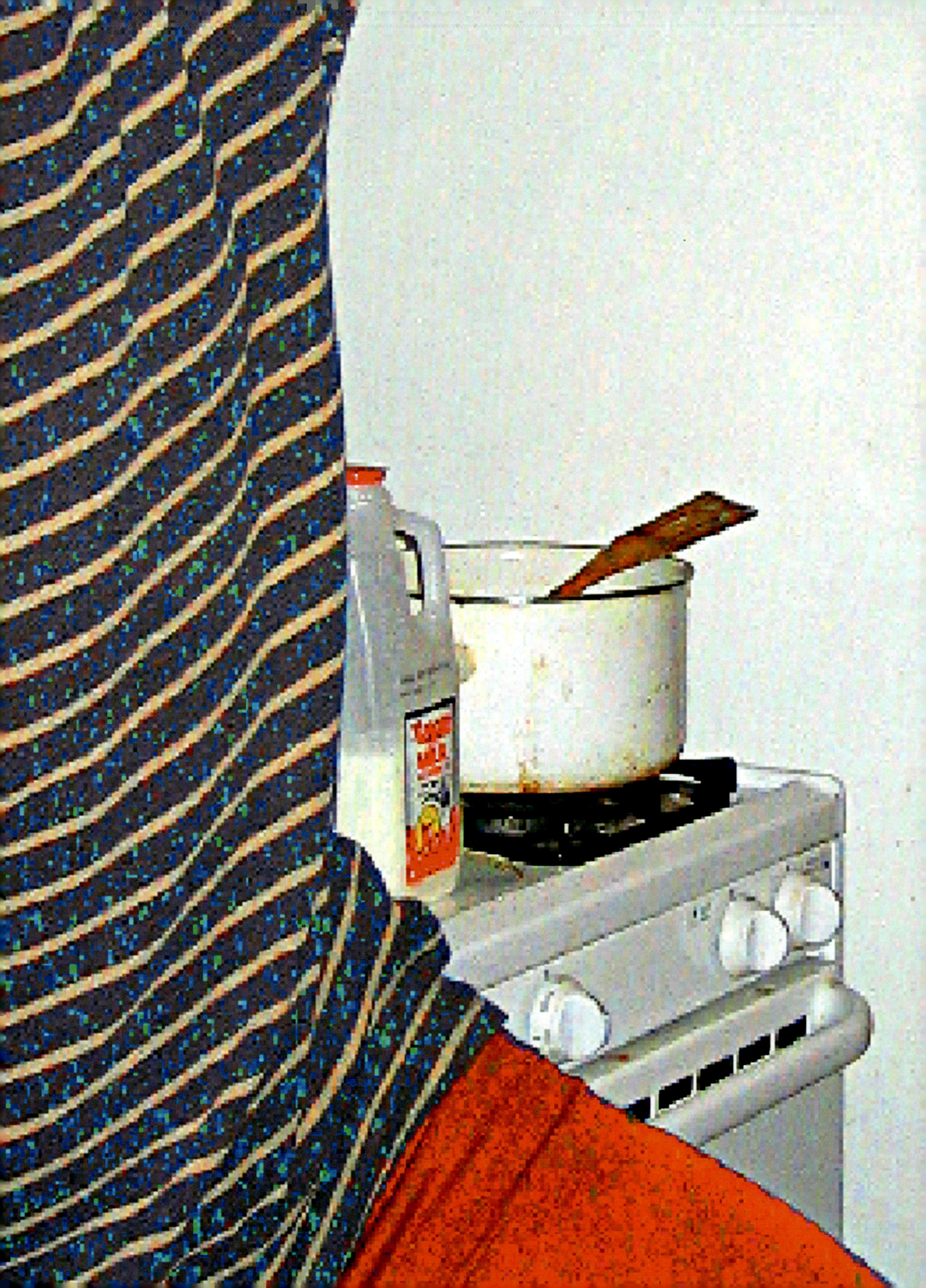

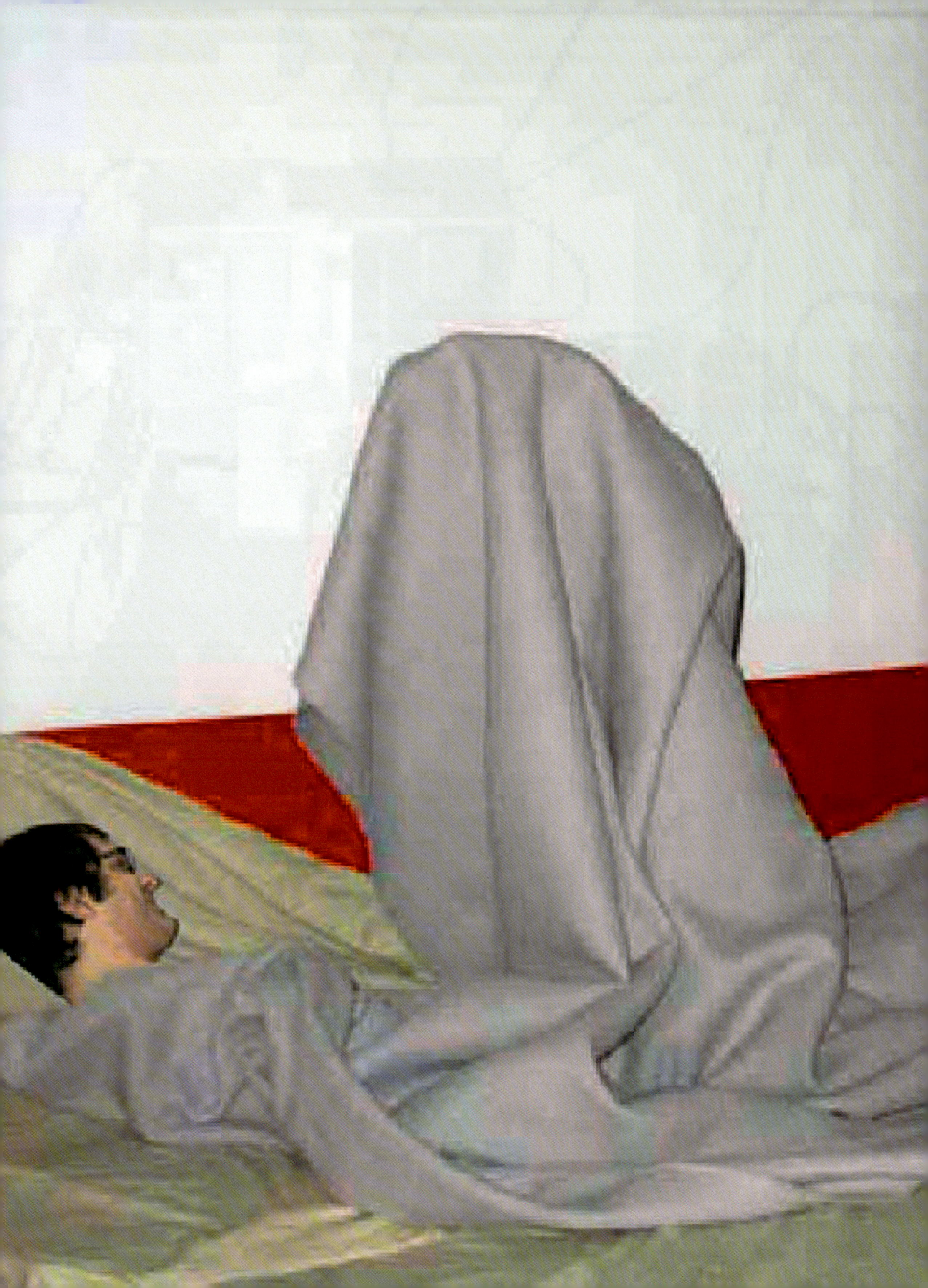

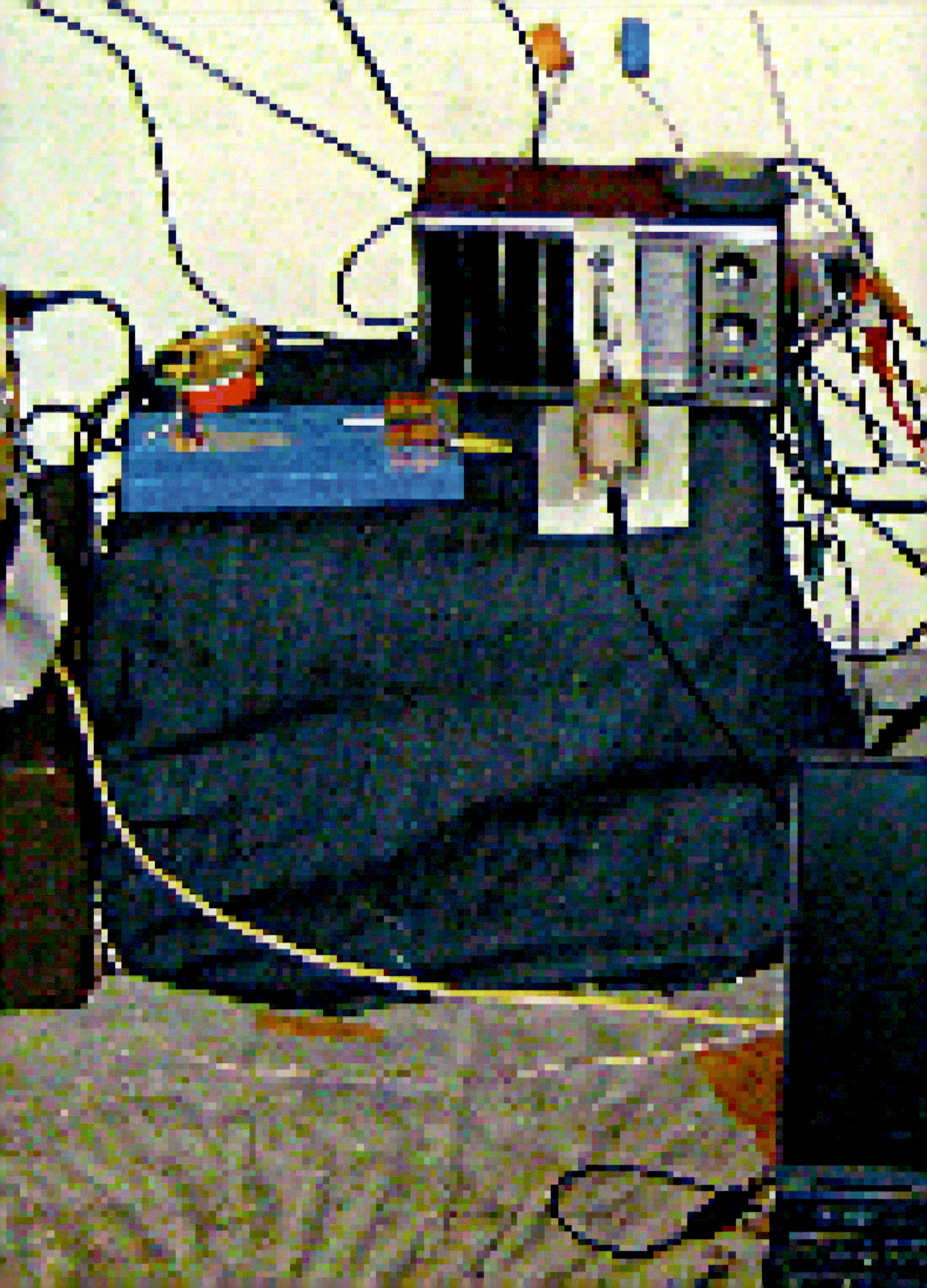

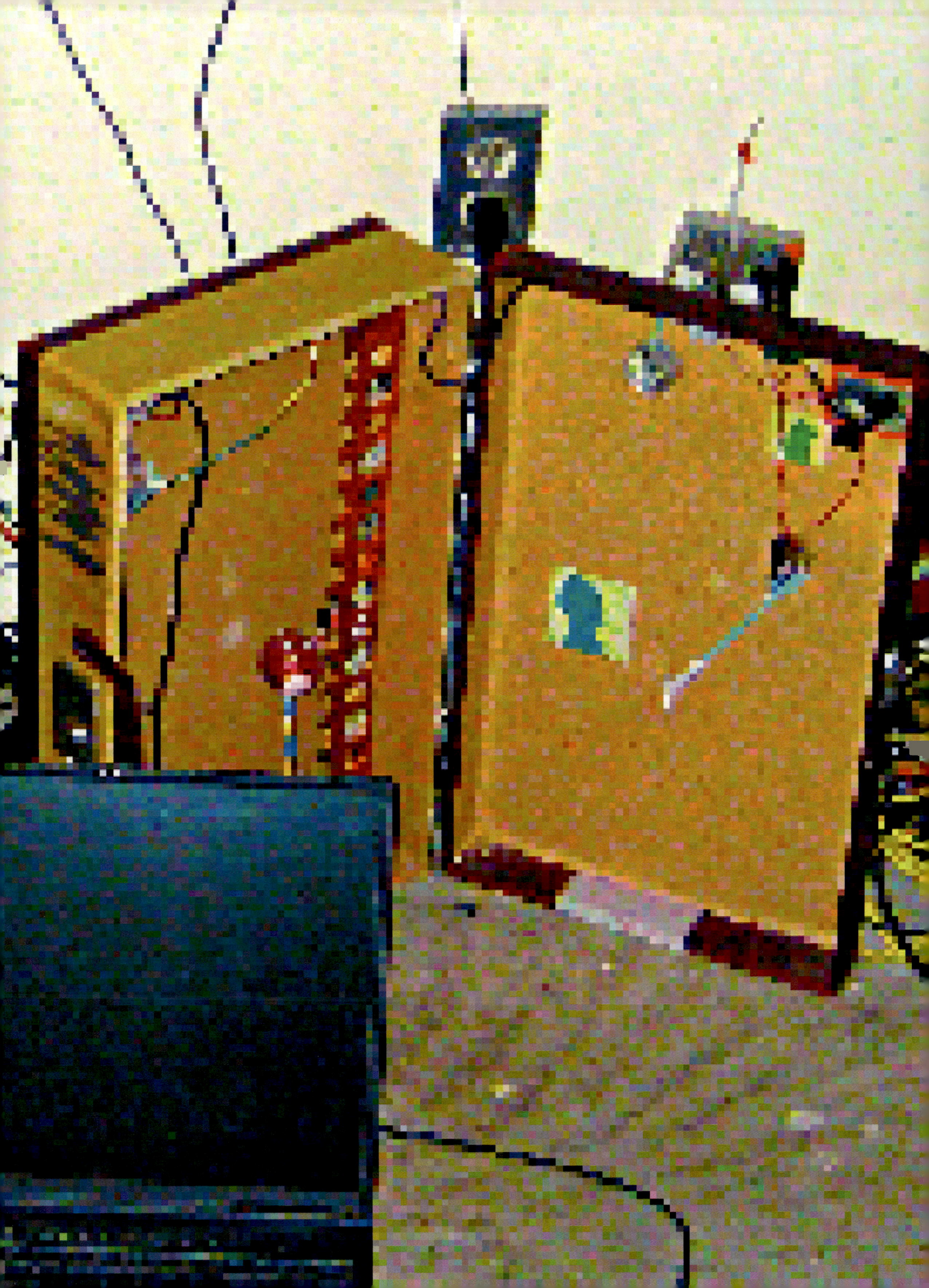

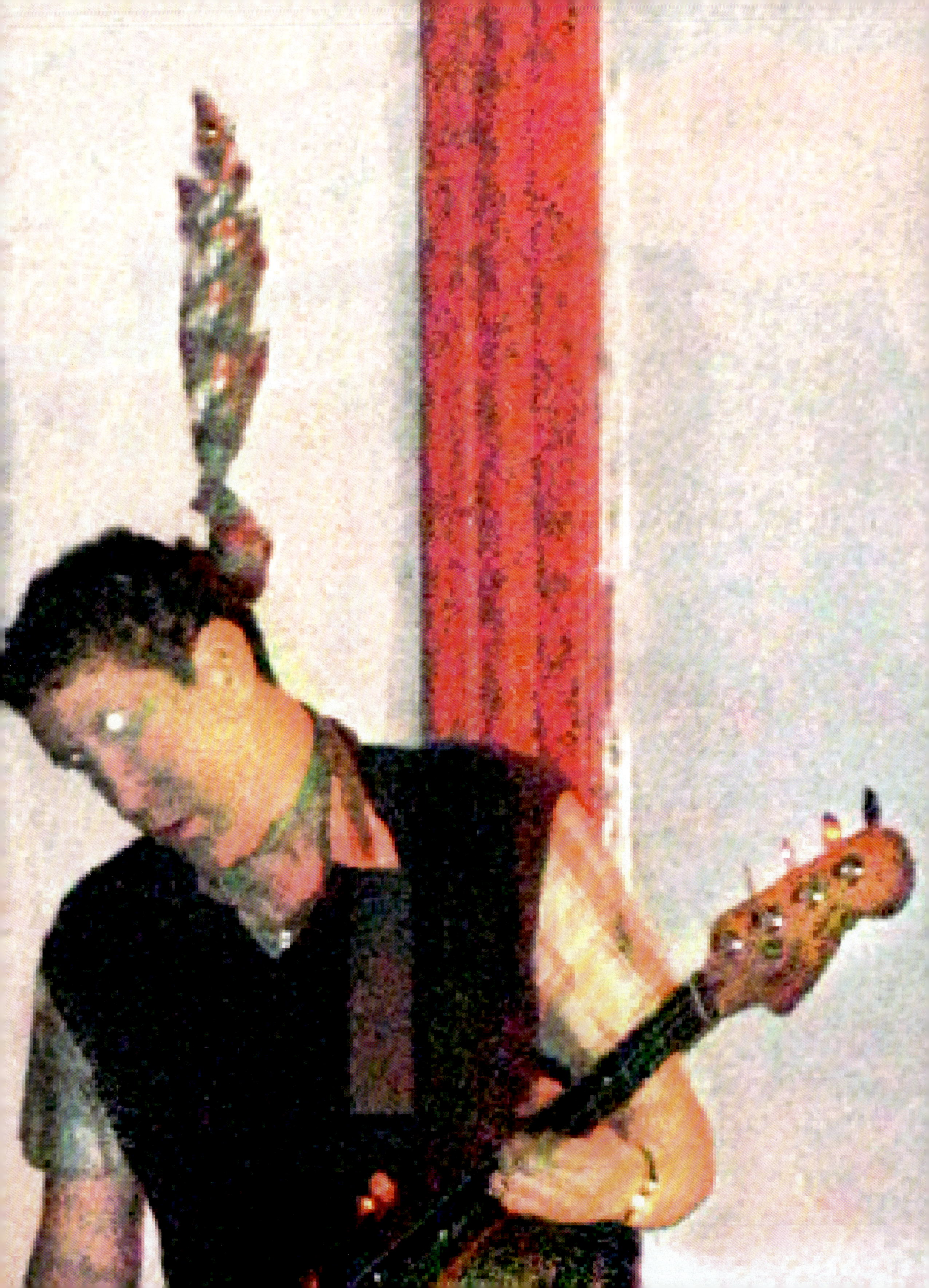

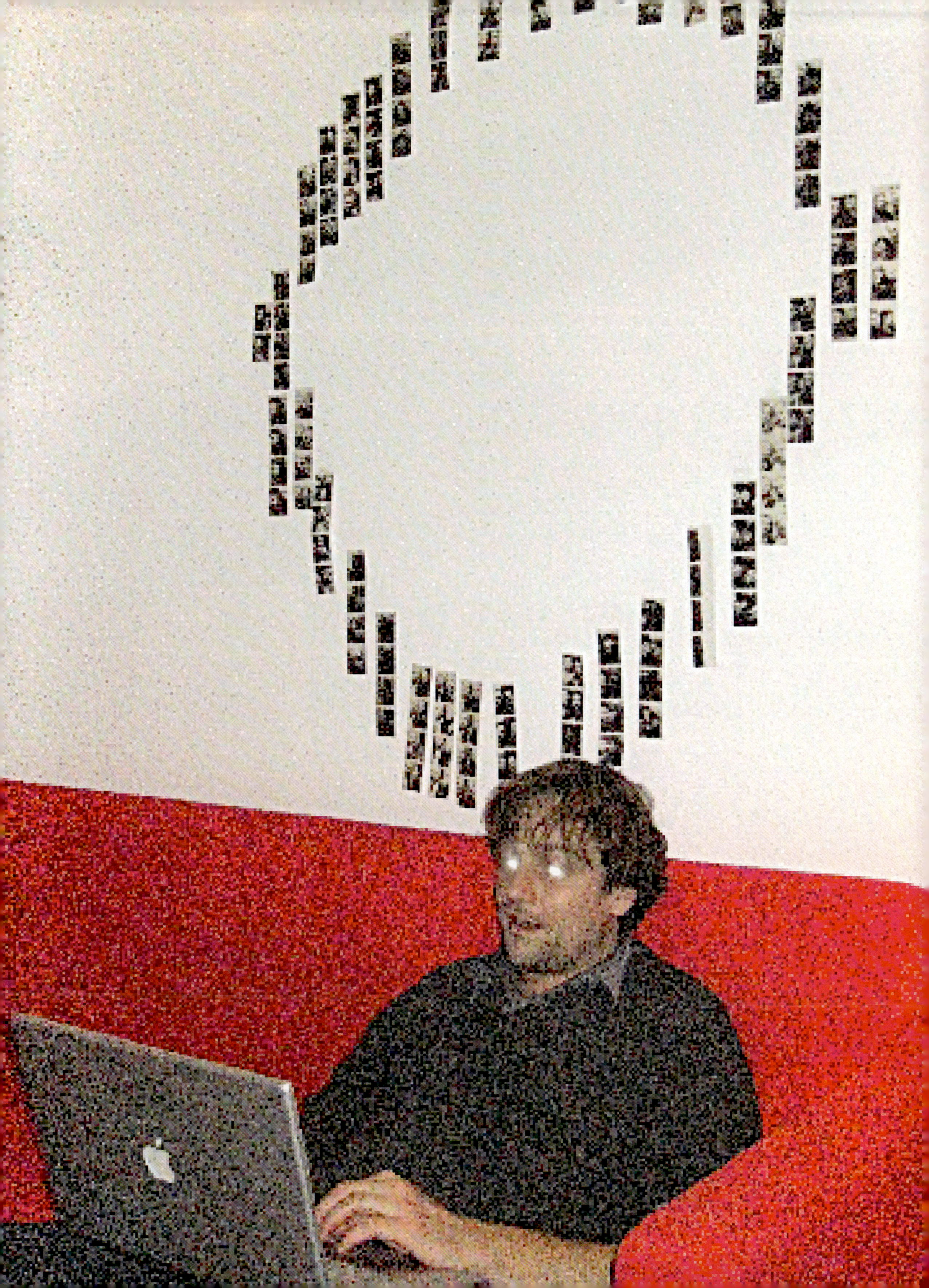

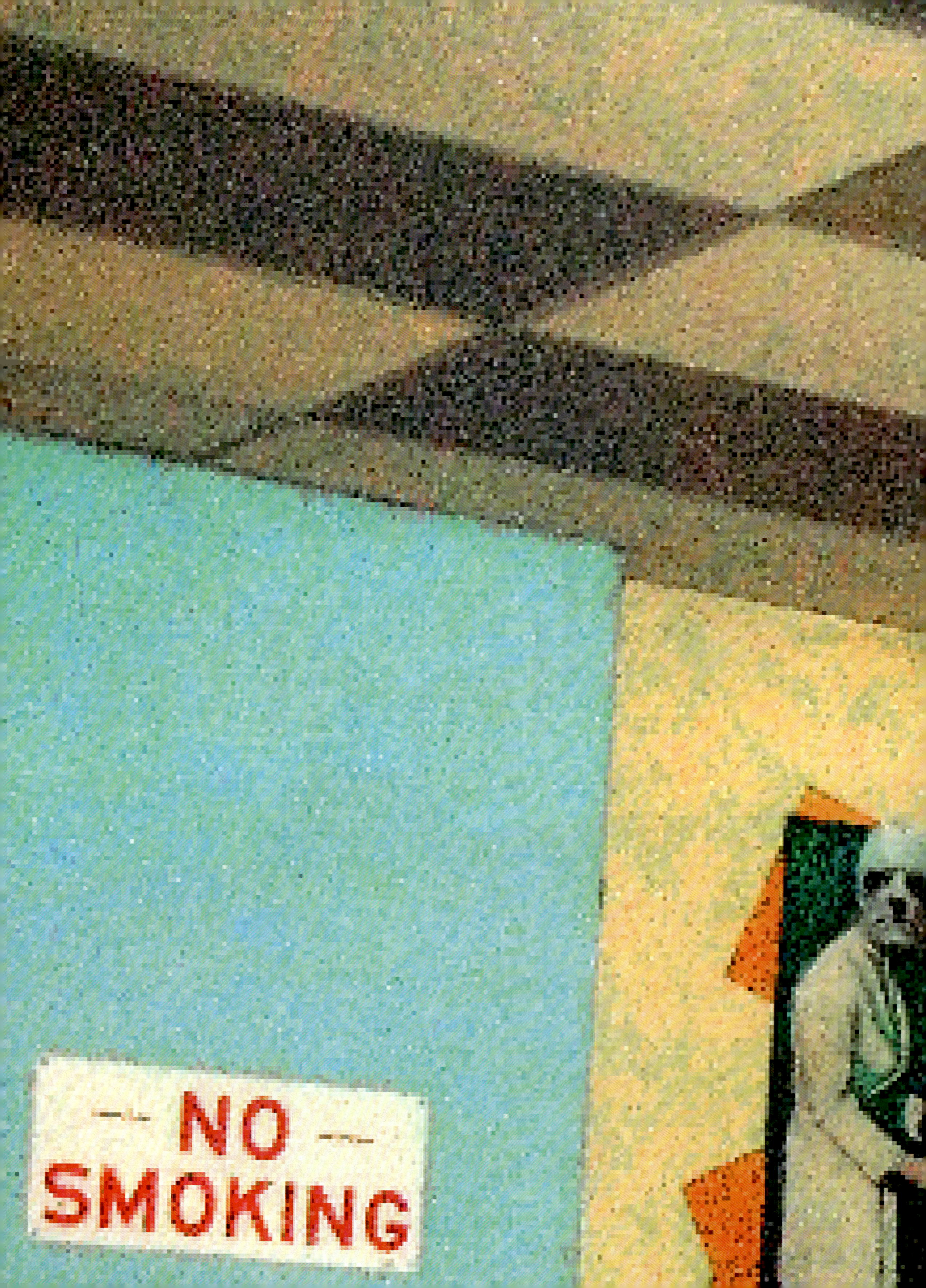
NO
SMOKING

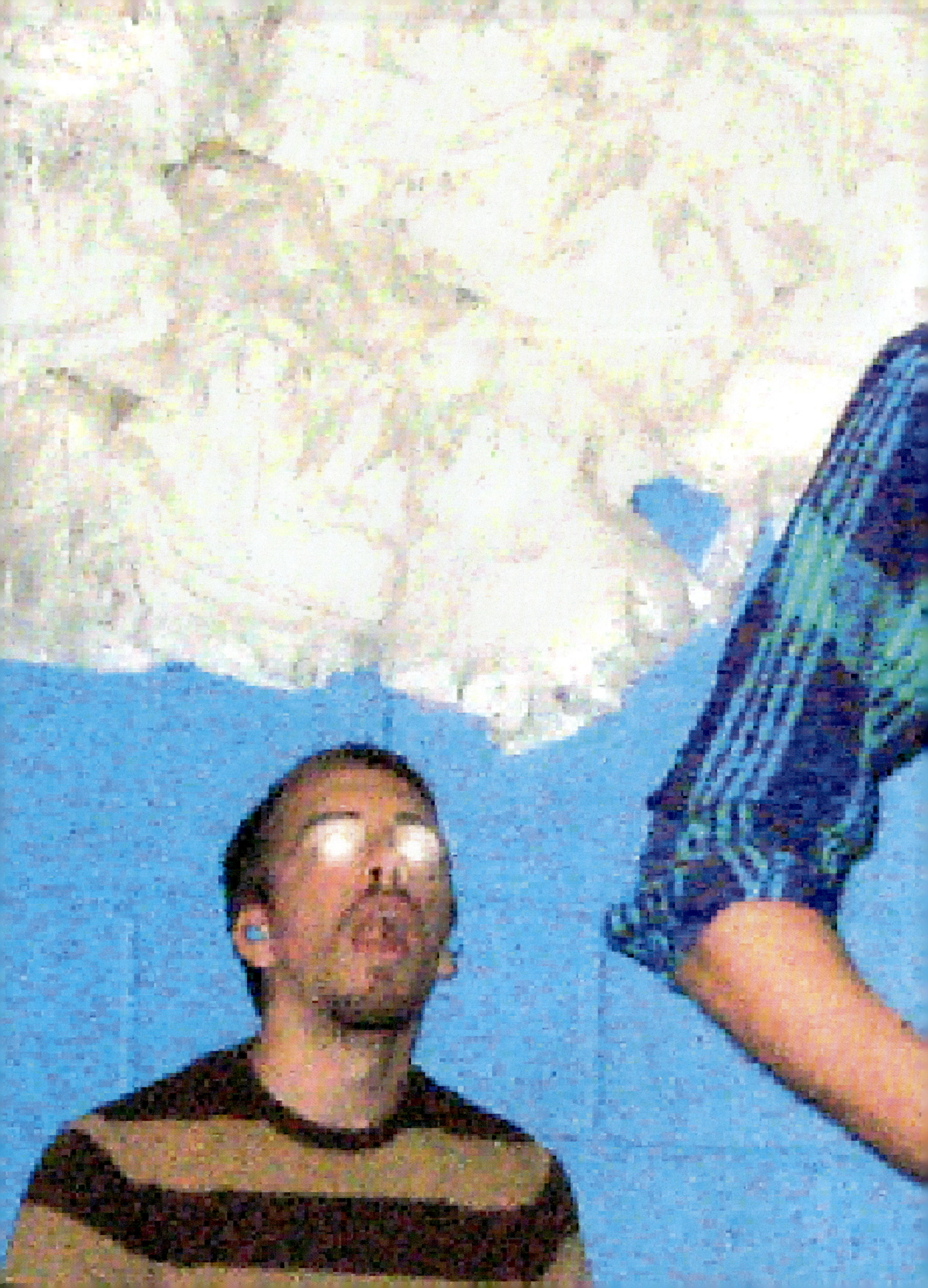

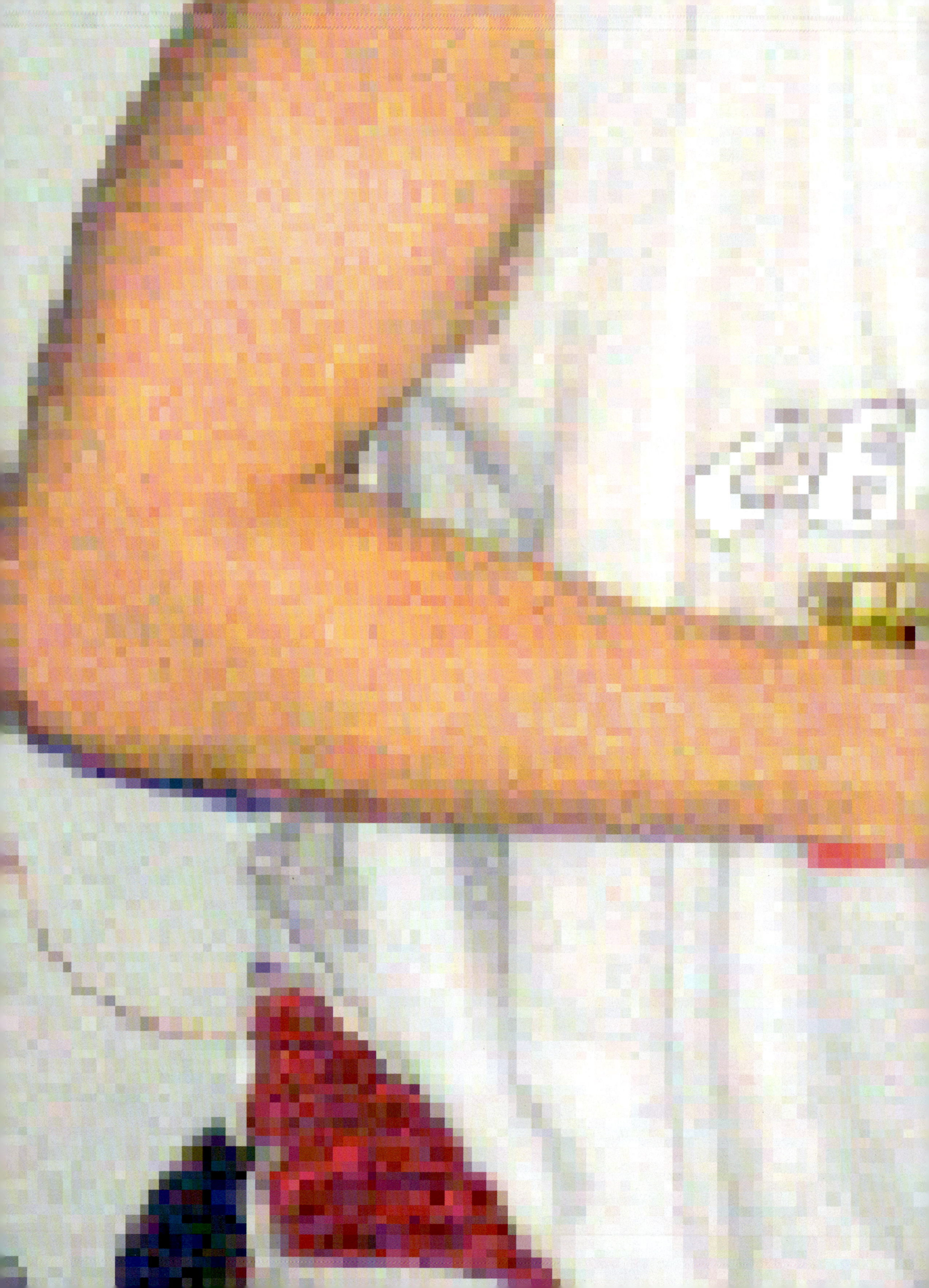

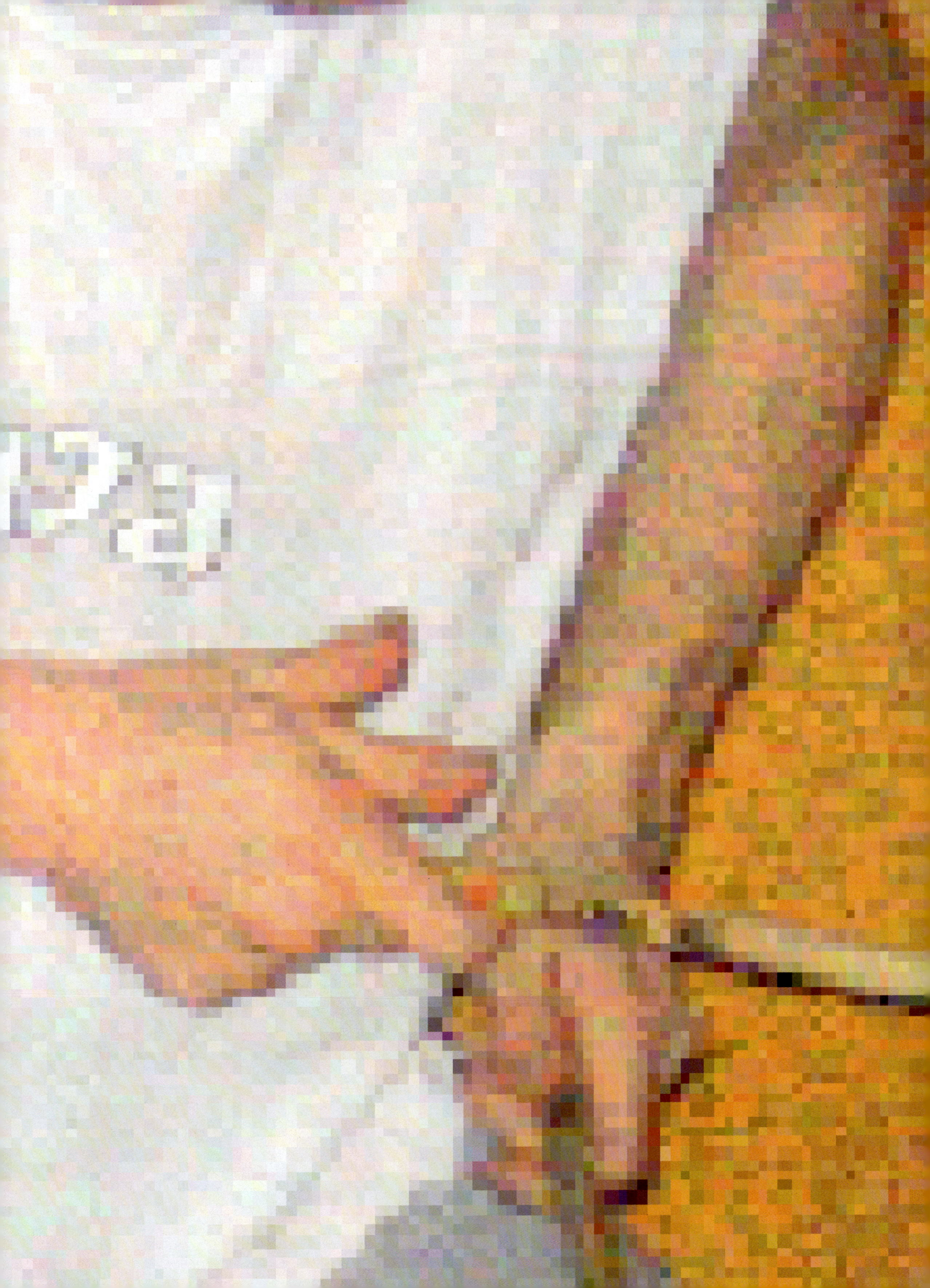

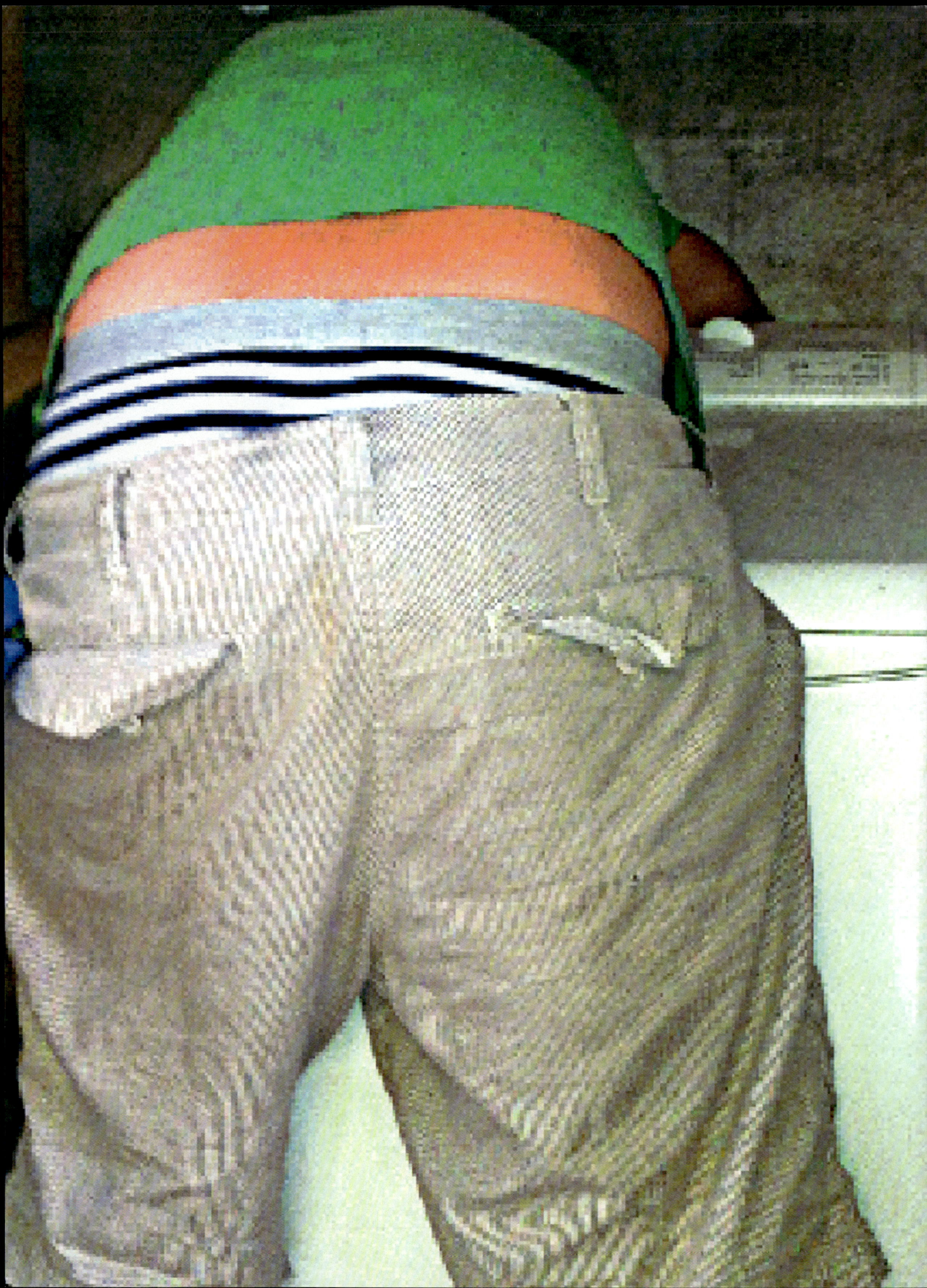

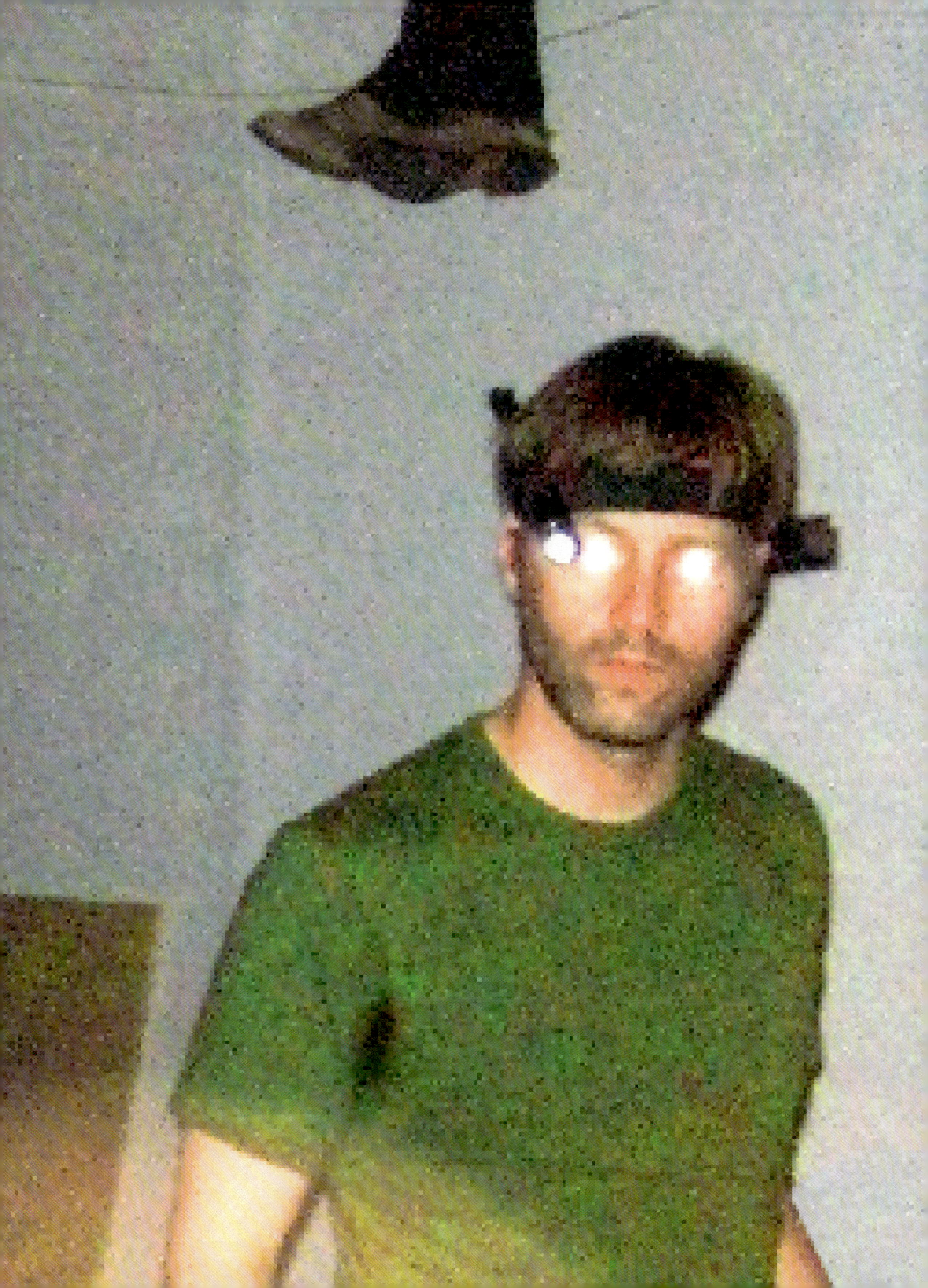

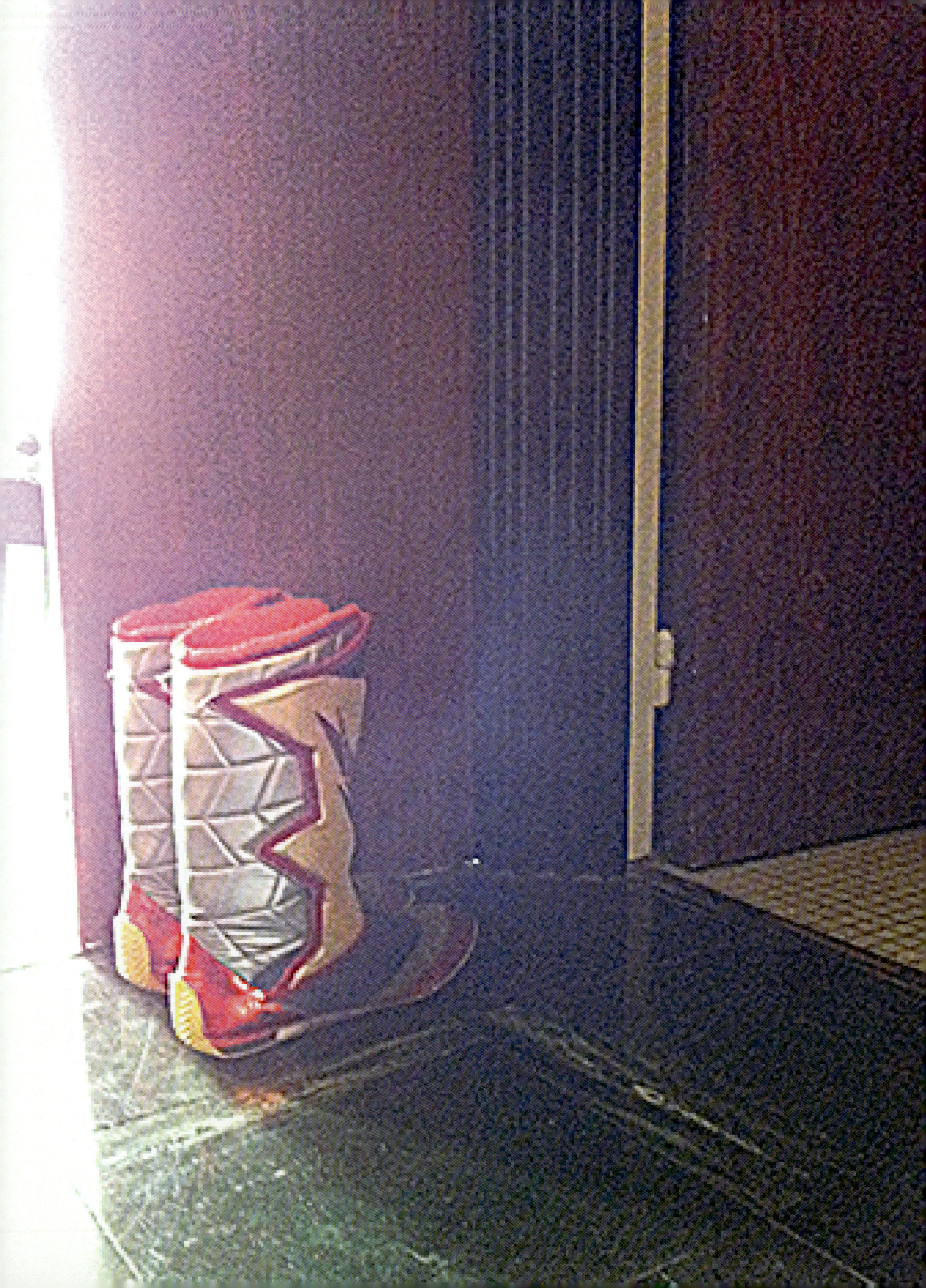

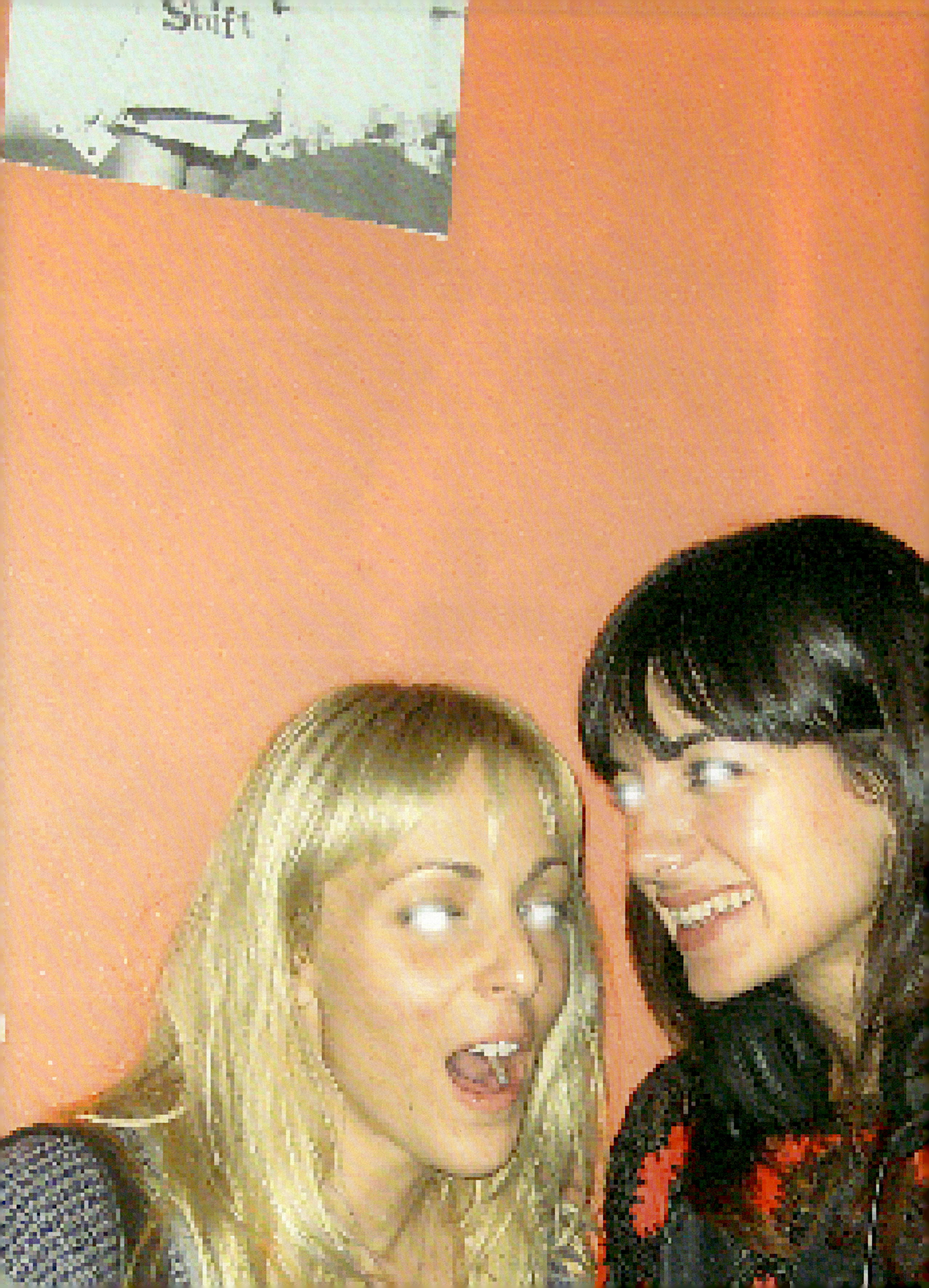
Shift

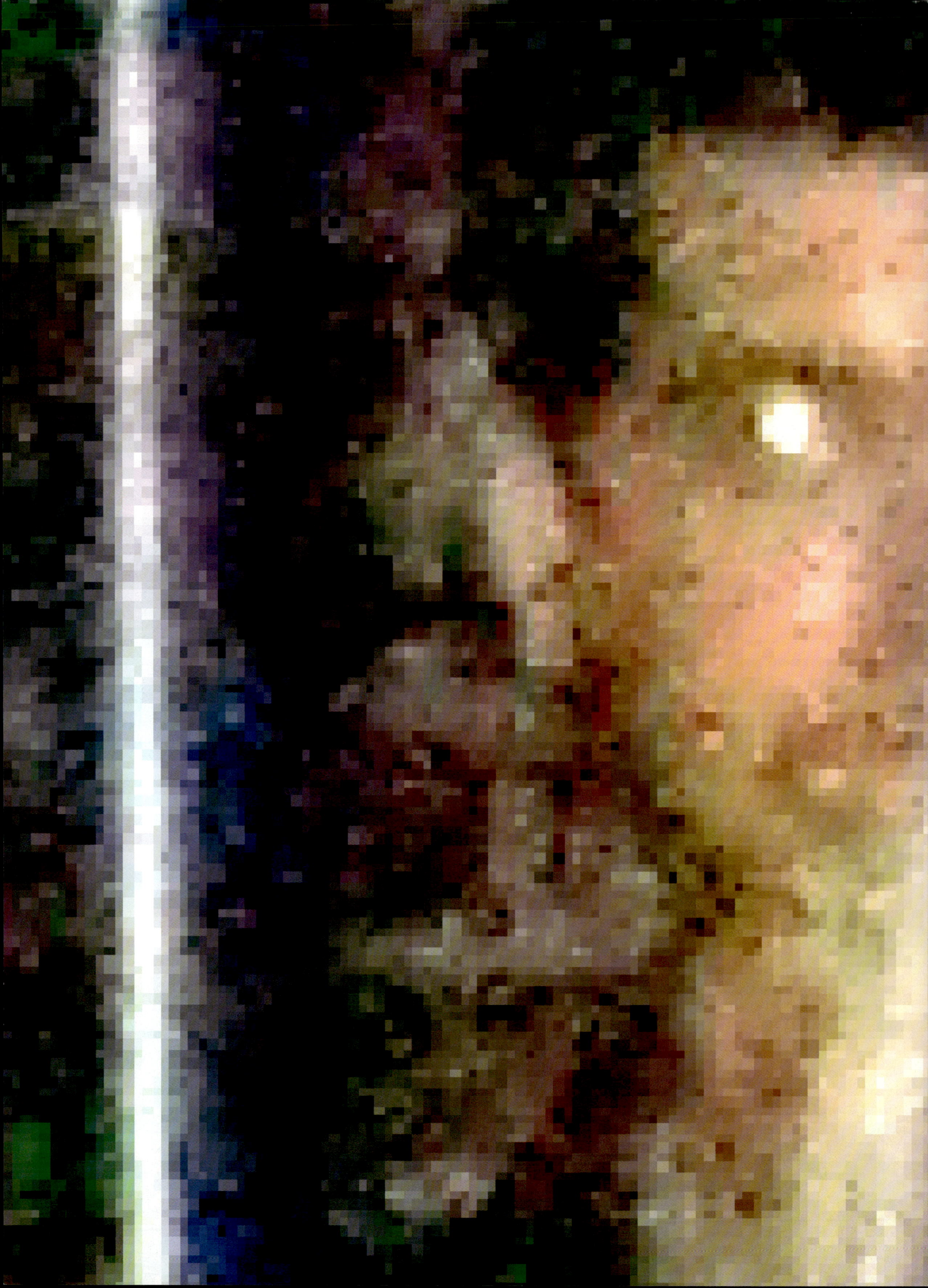

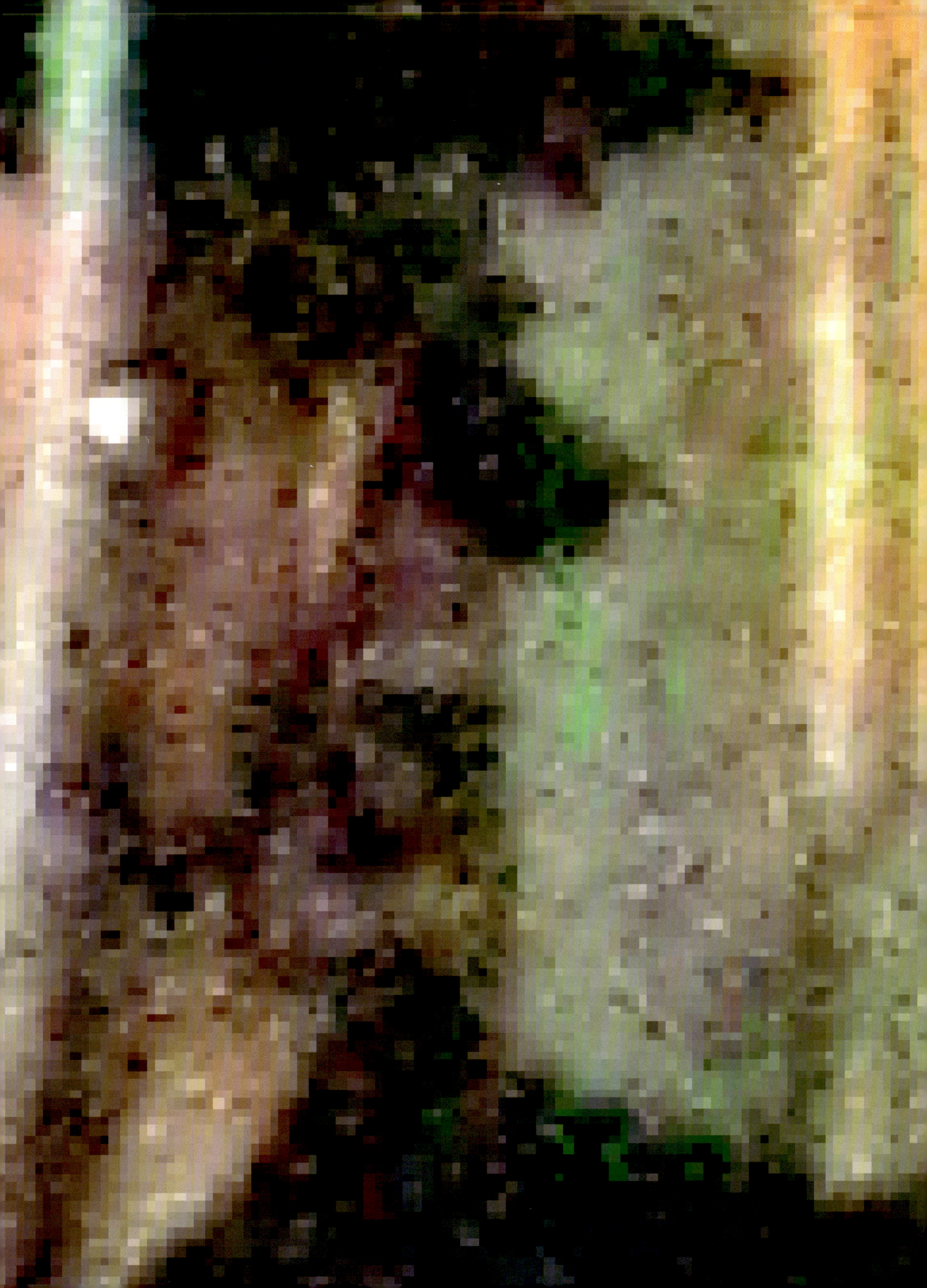

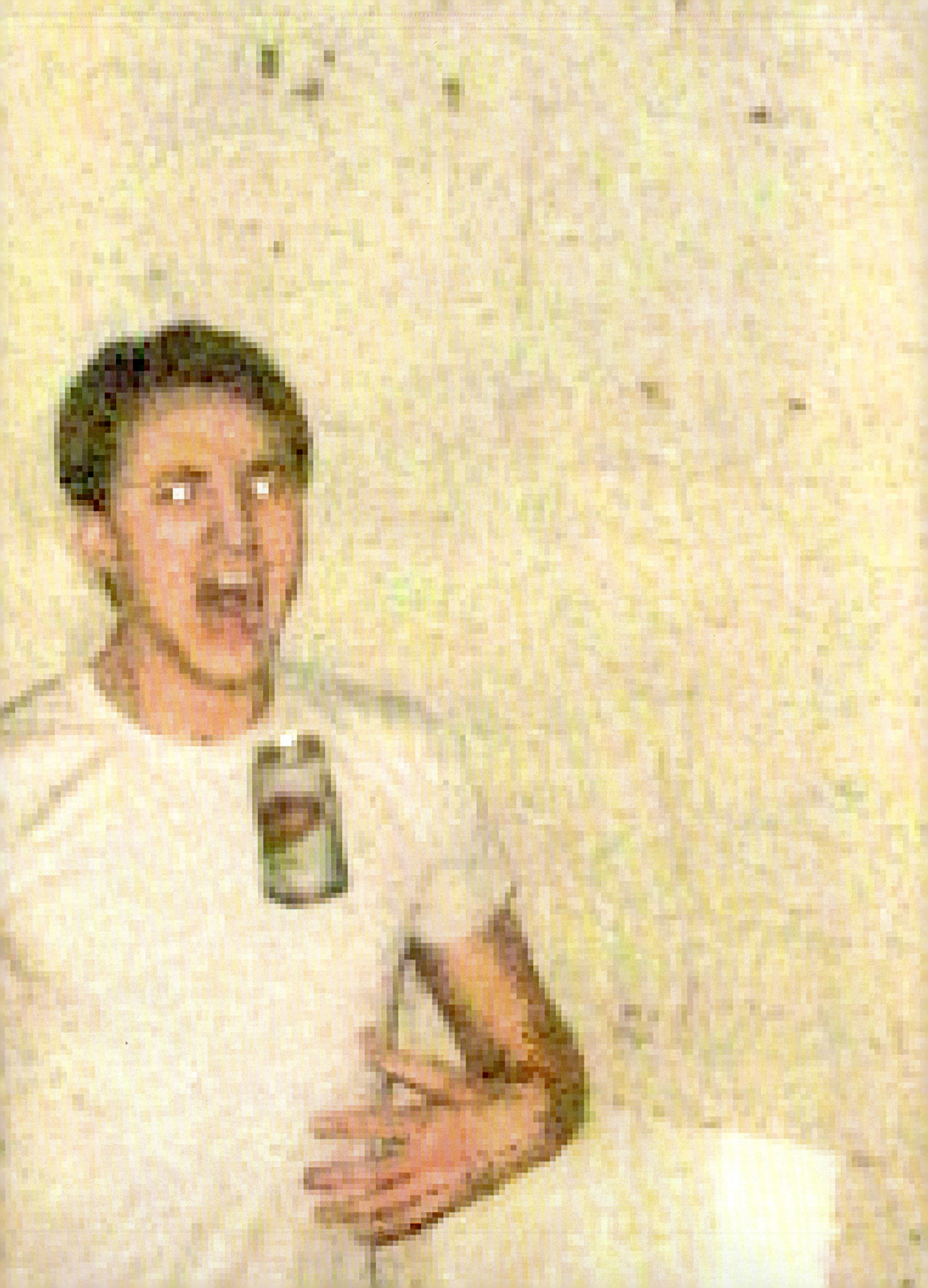

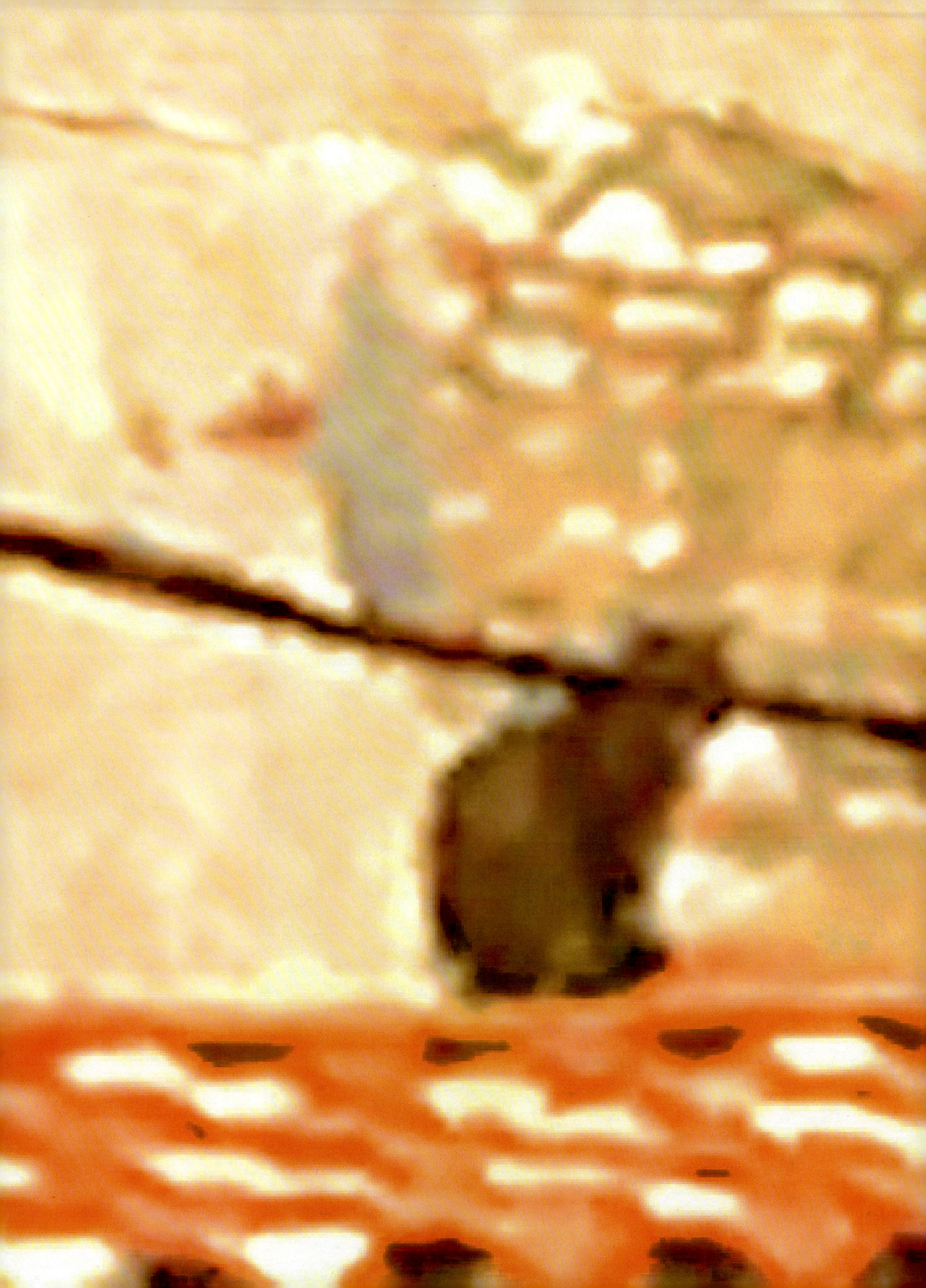

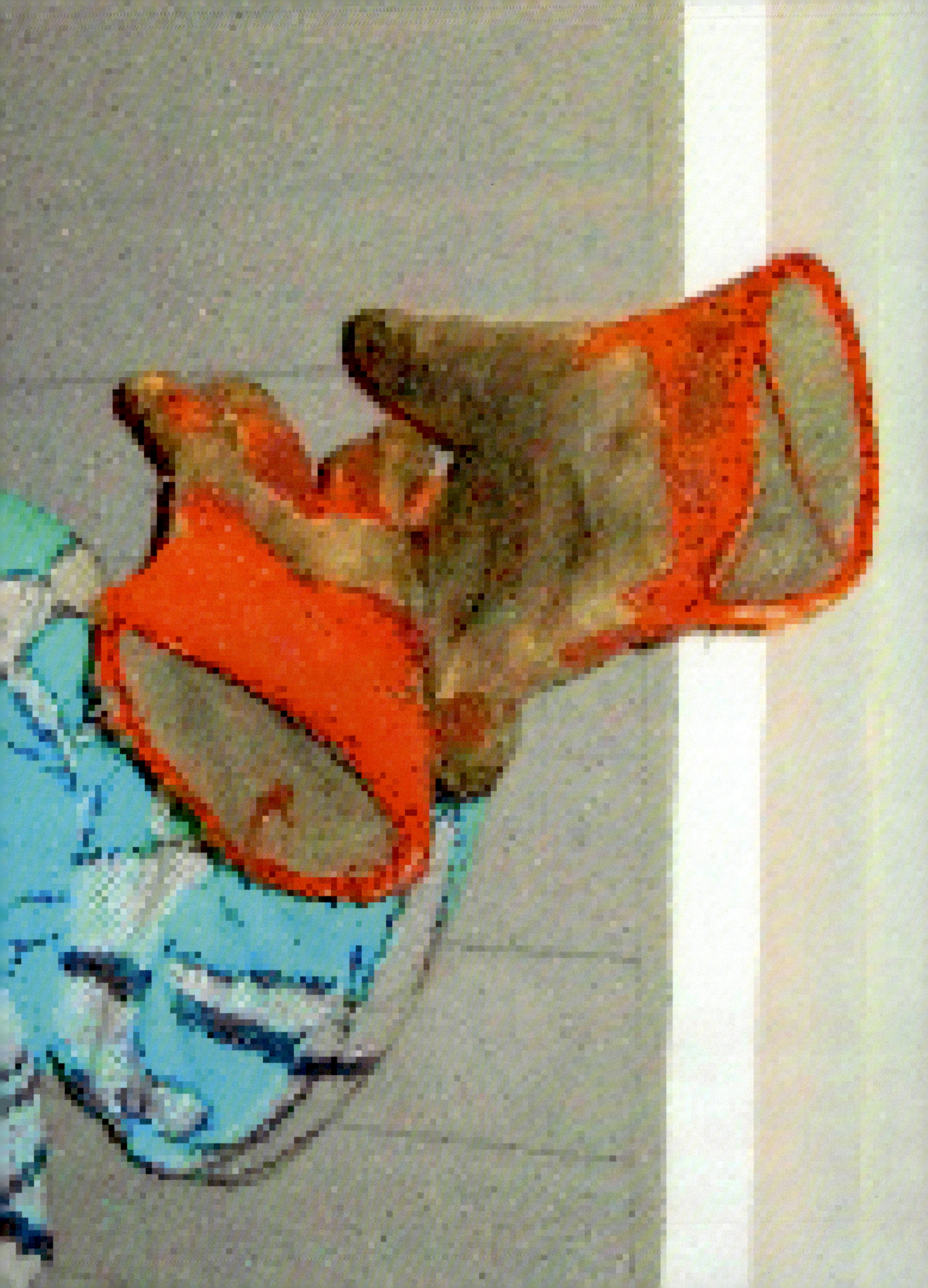

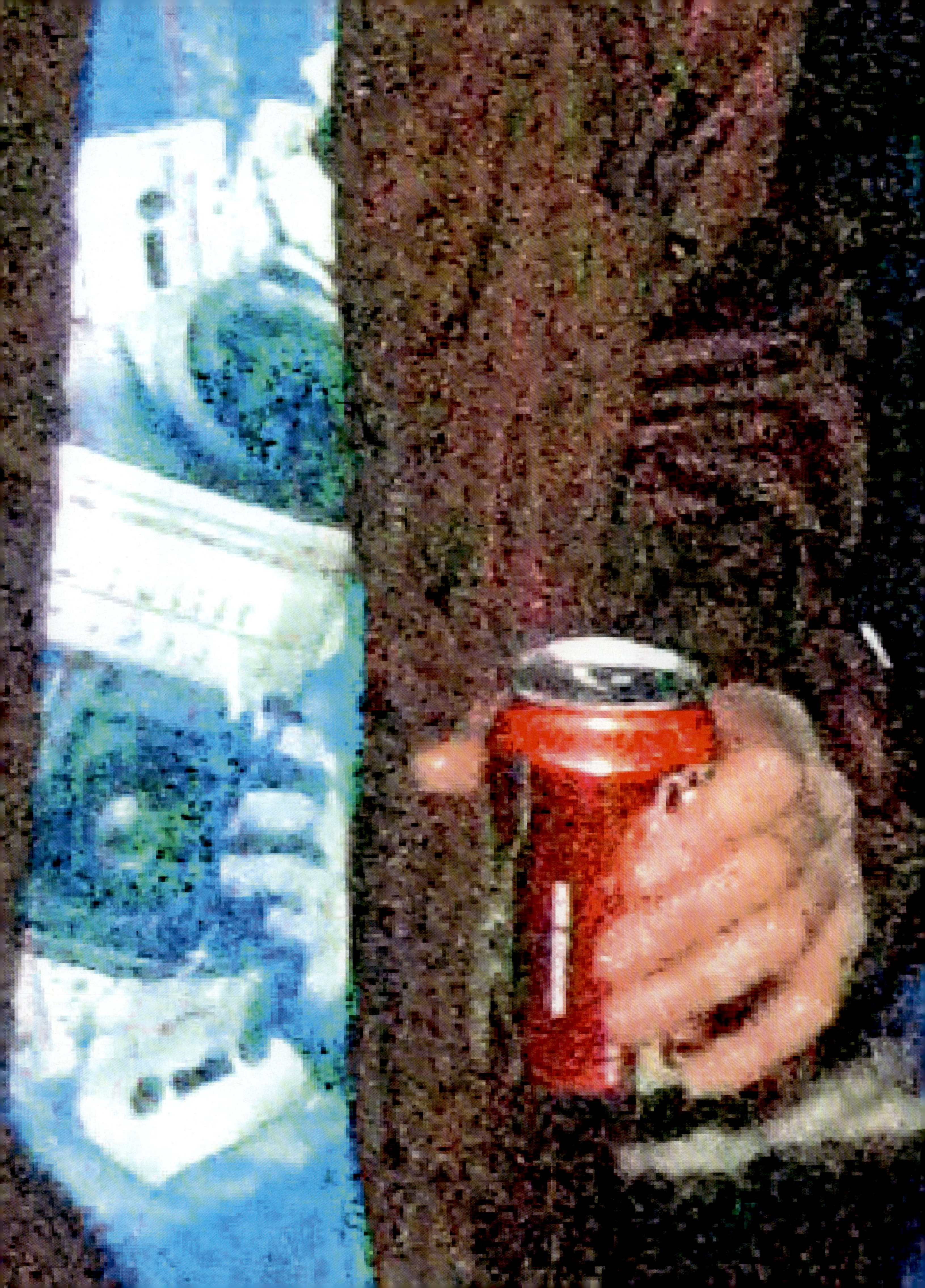

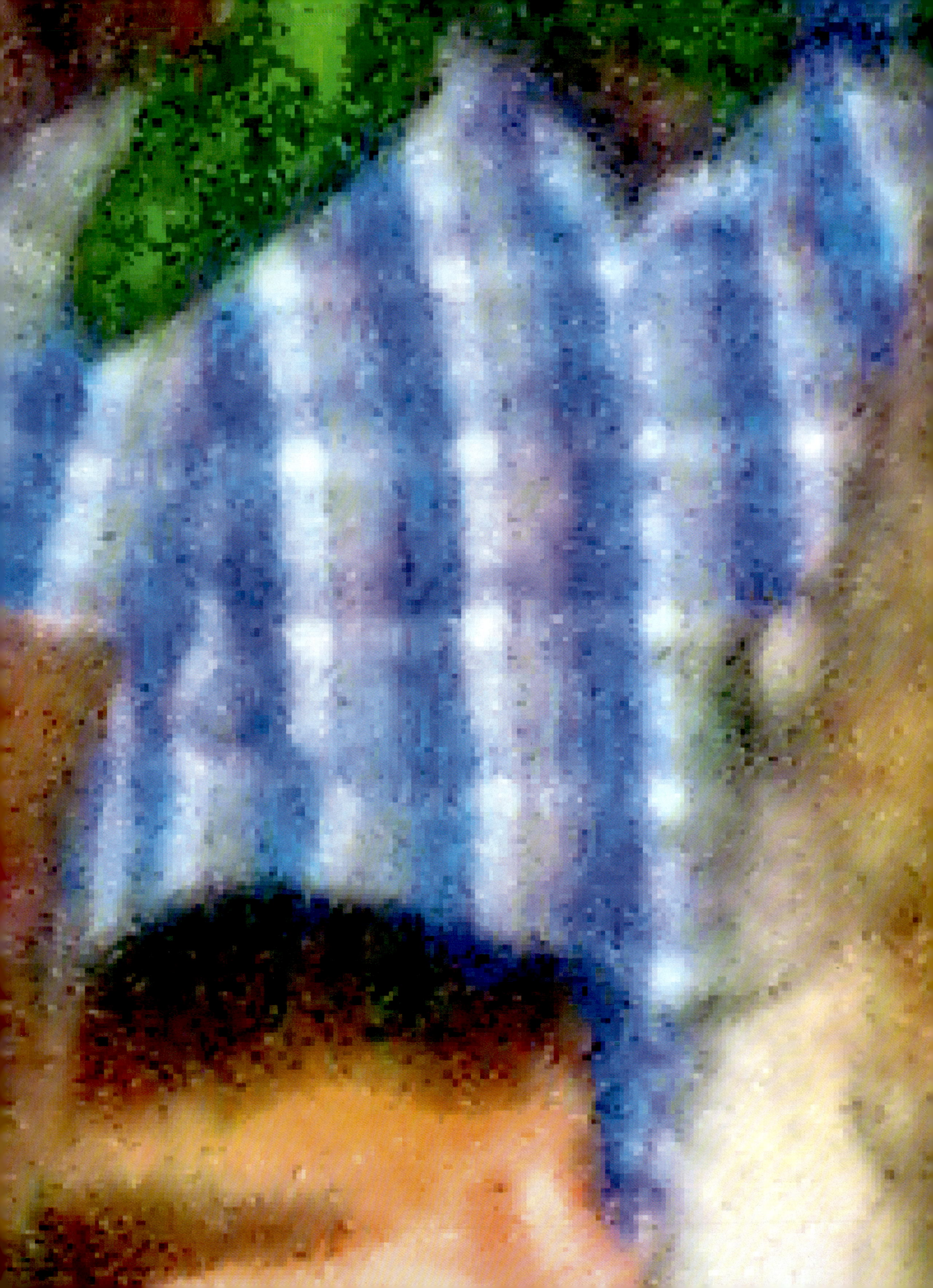

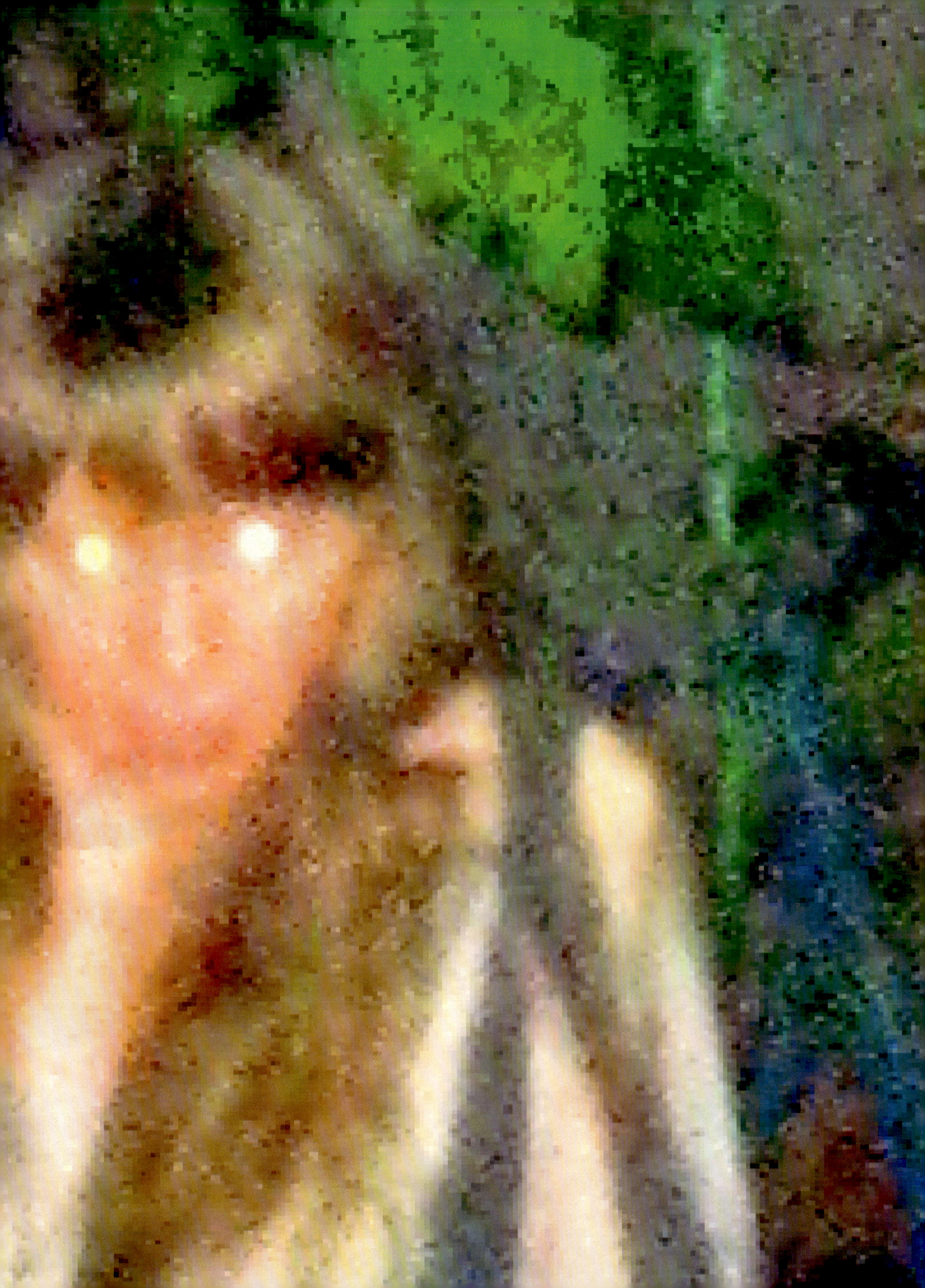

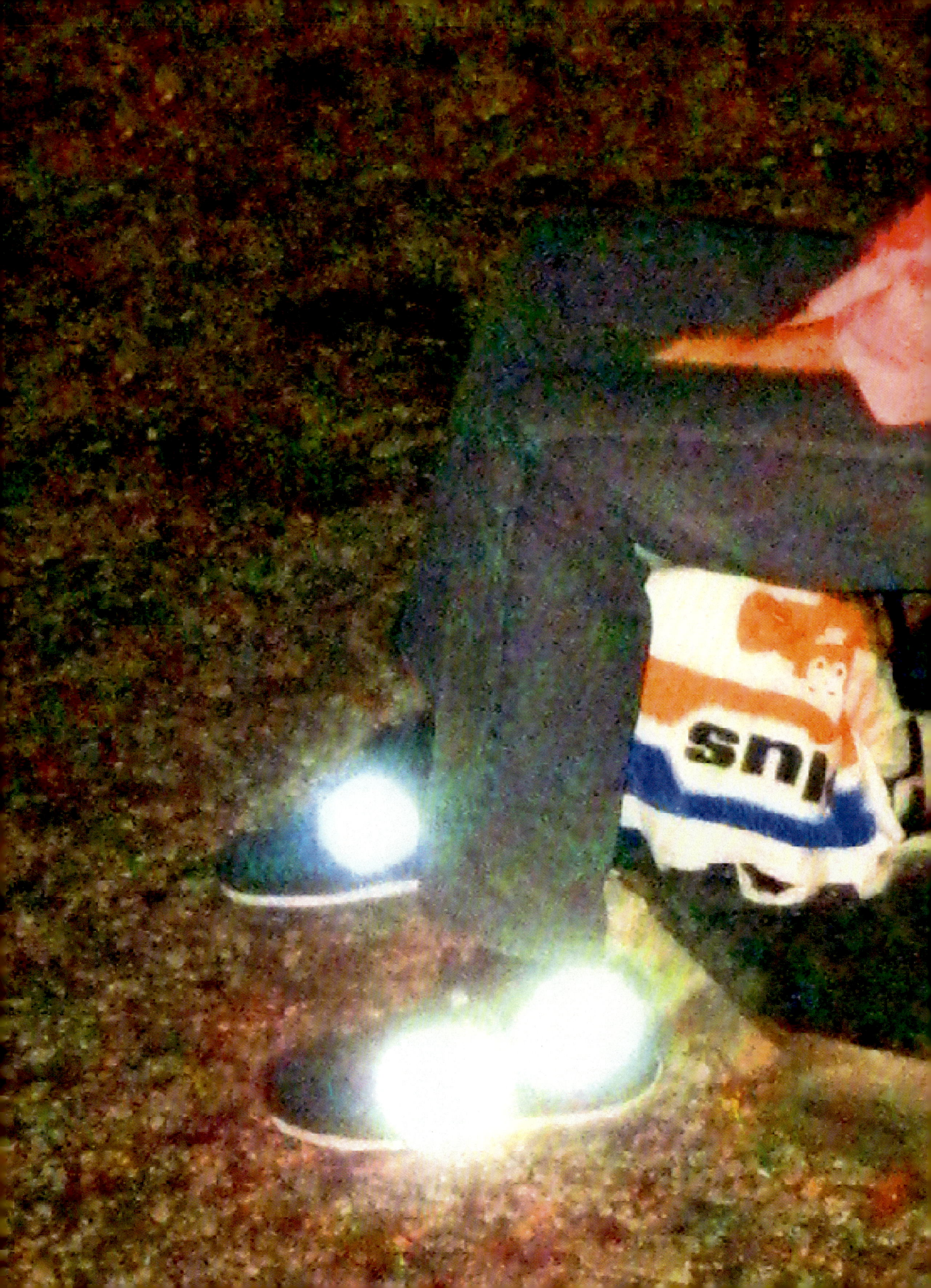

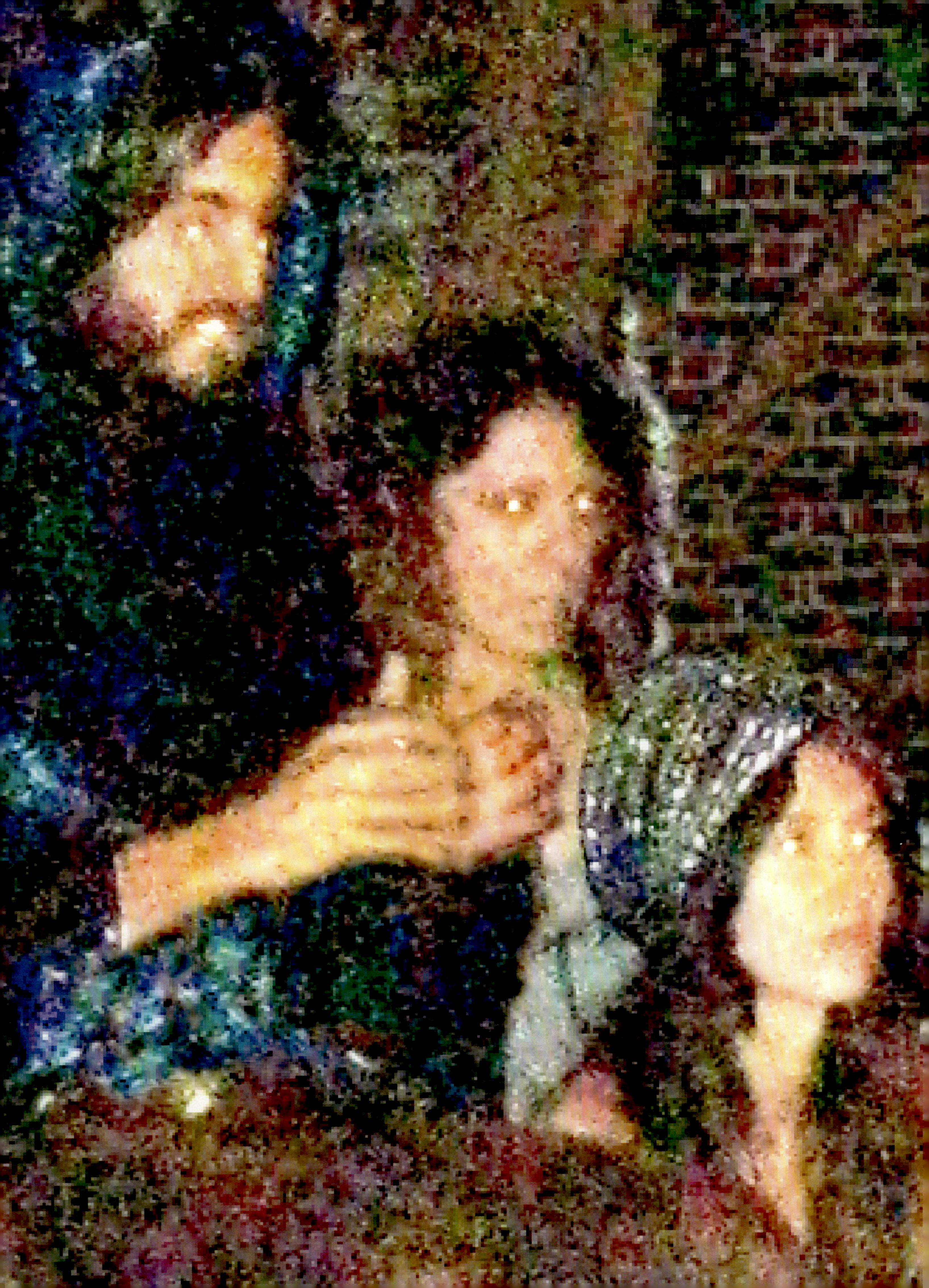

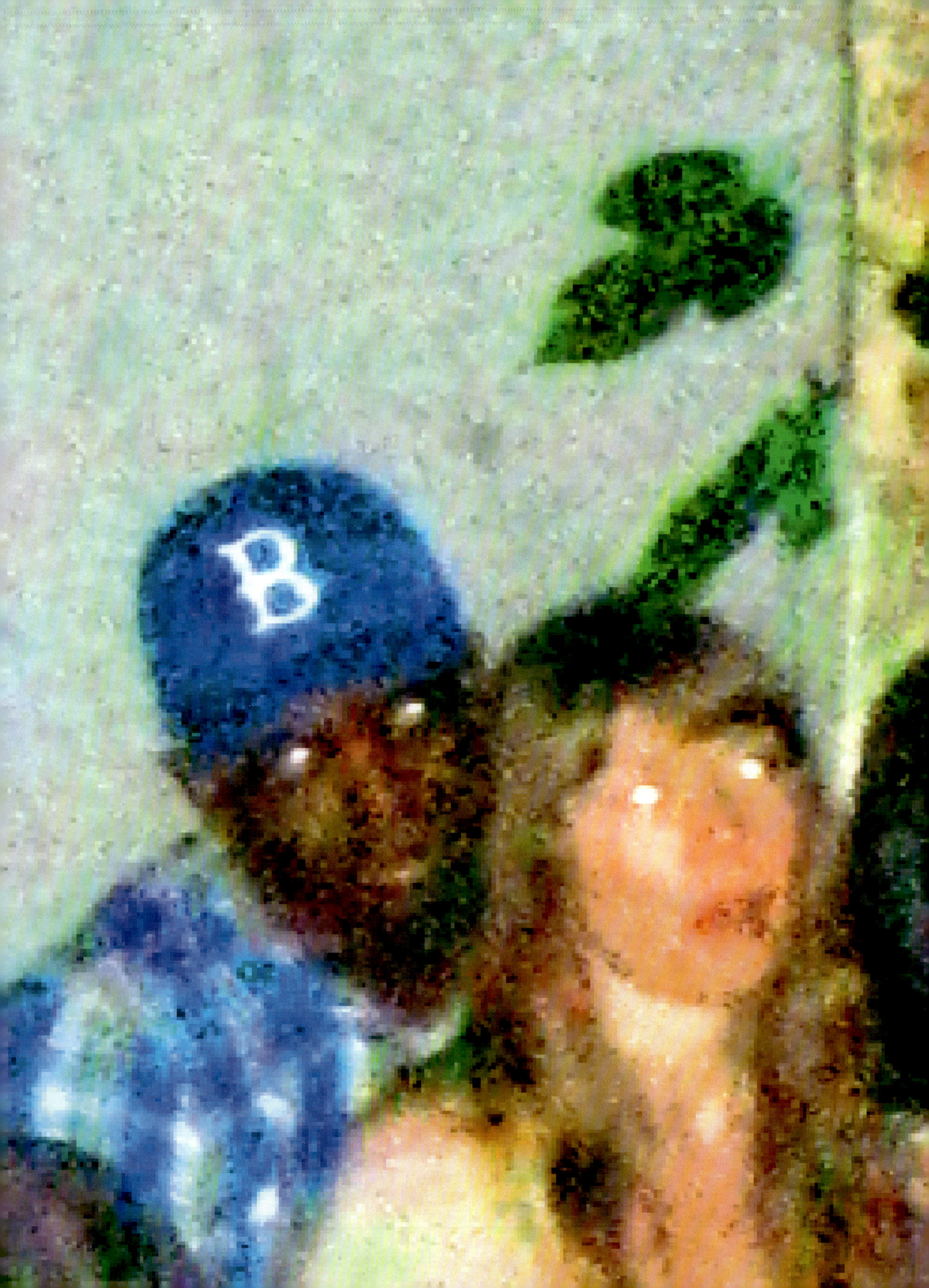

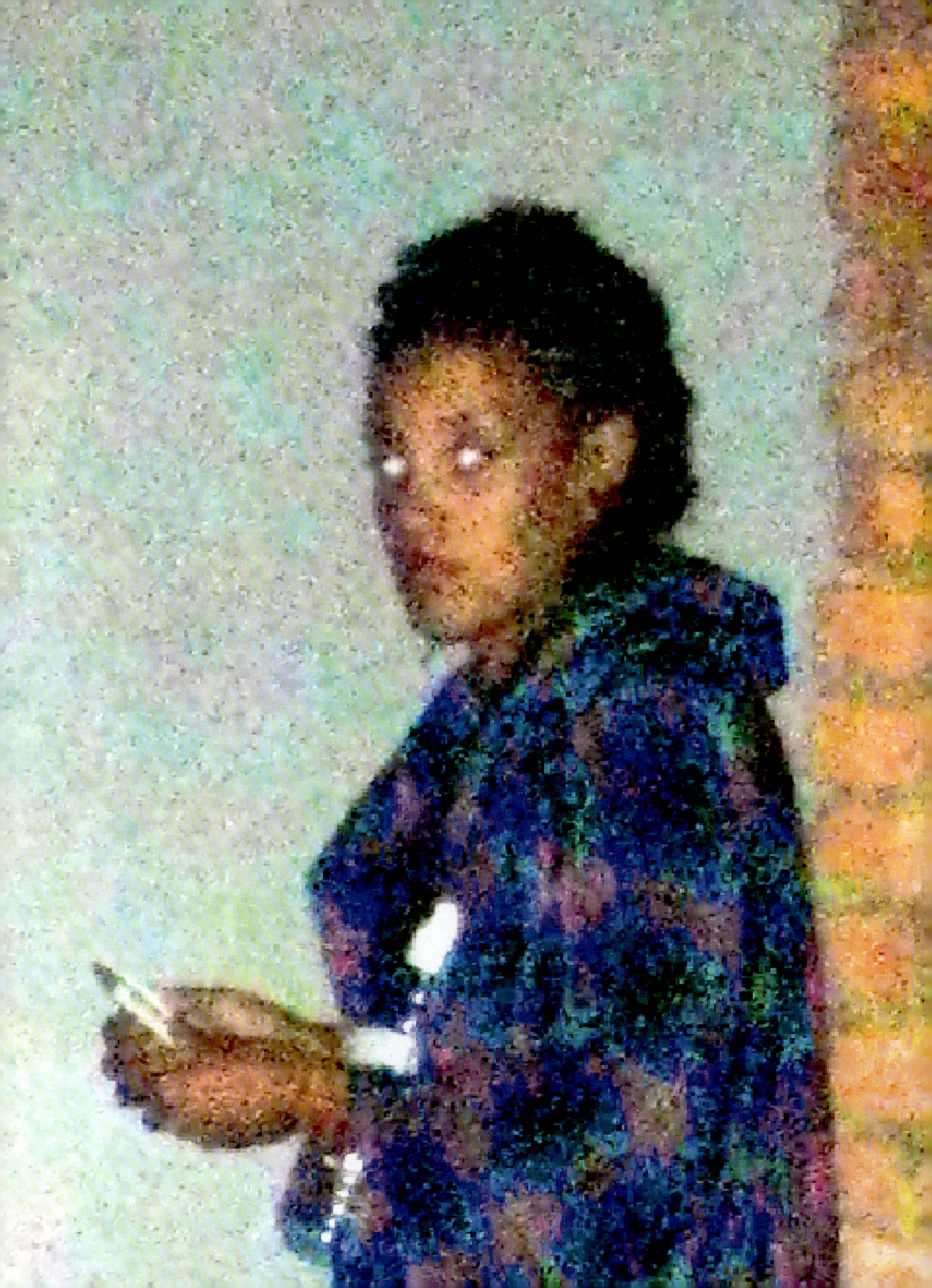

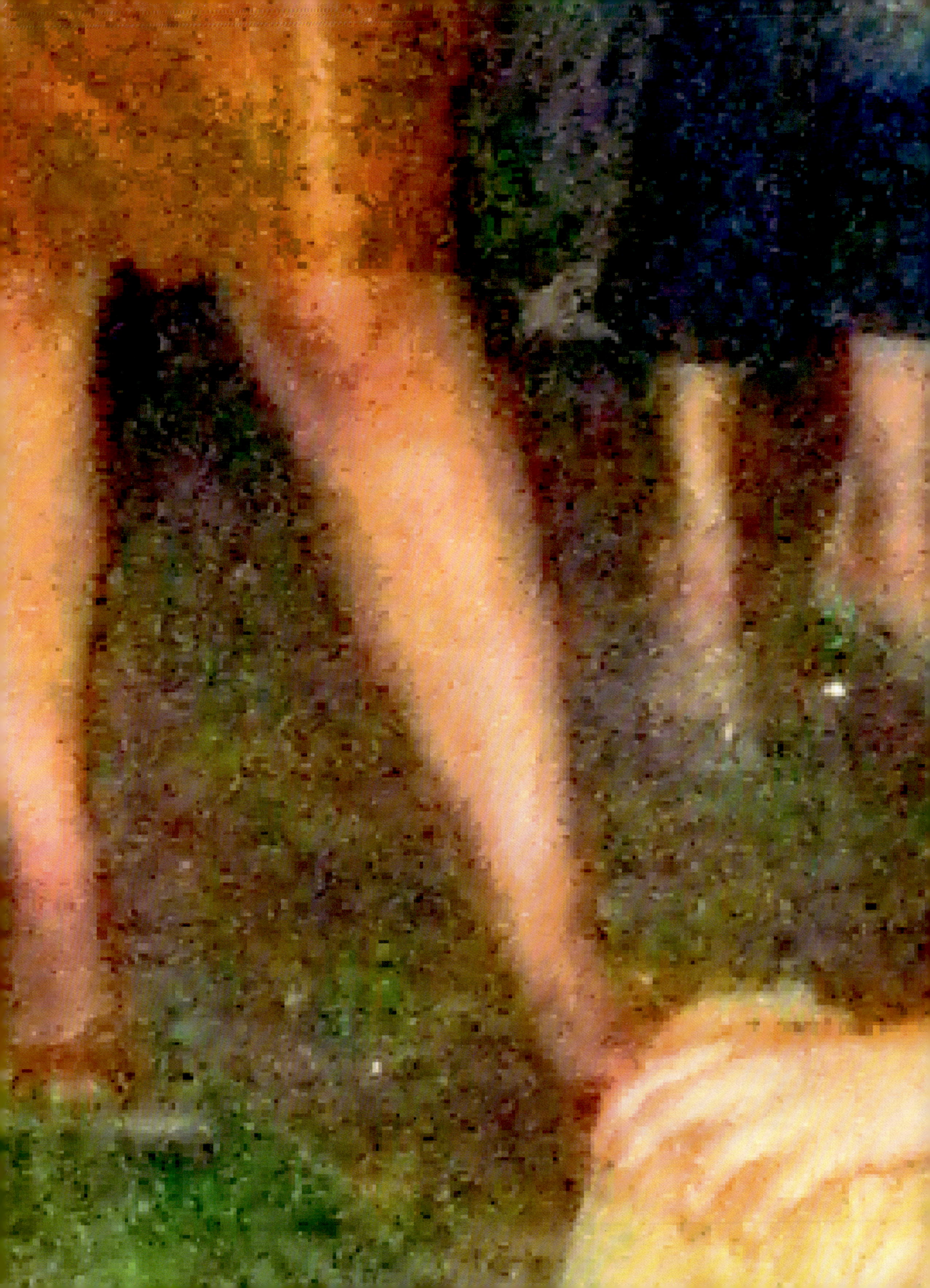

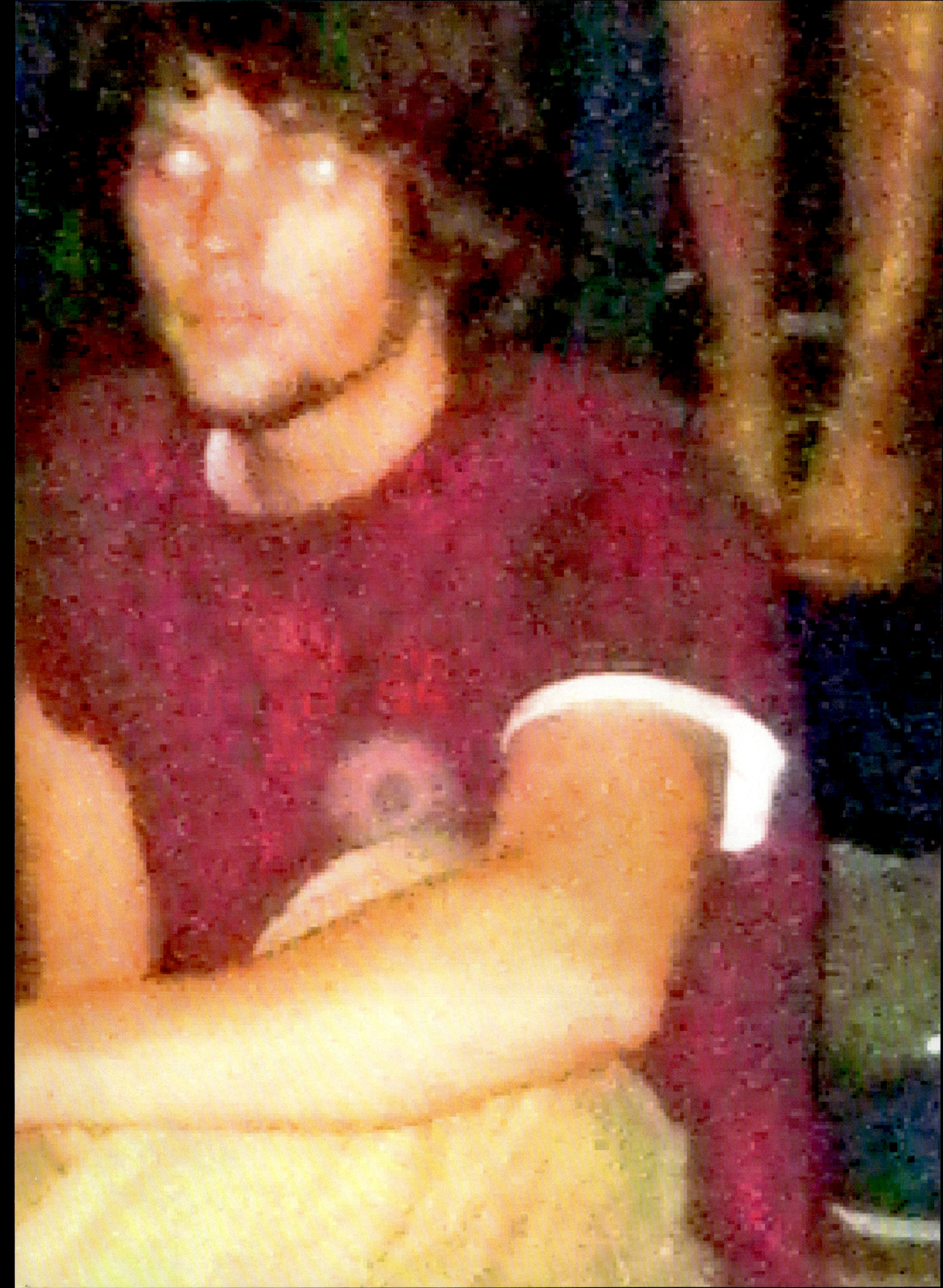

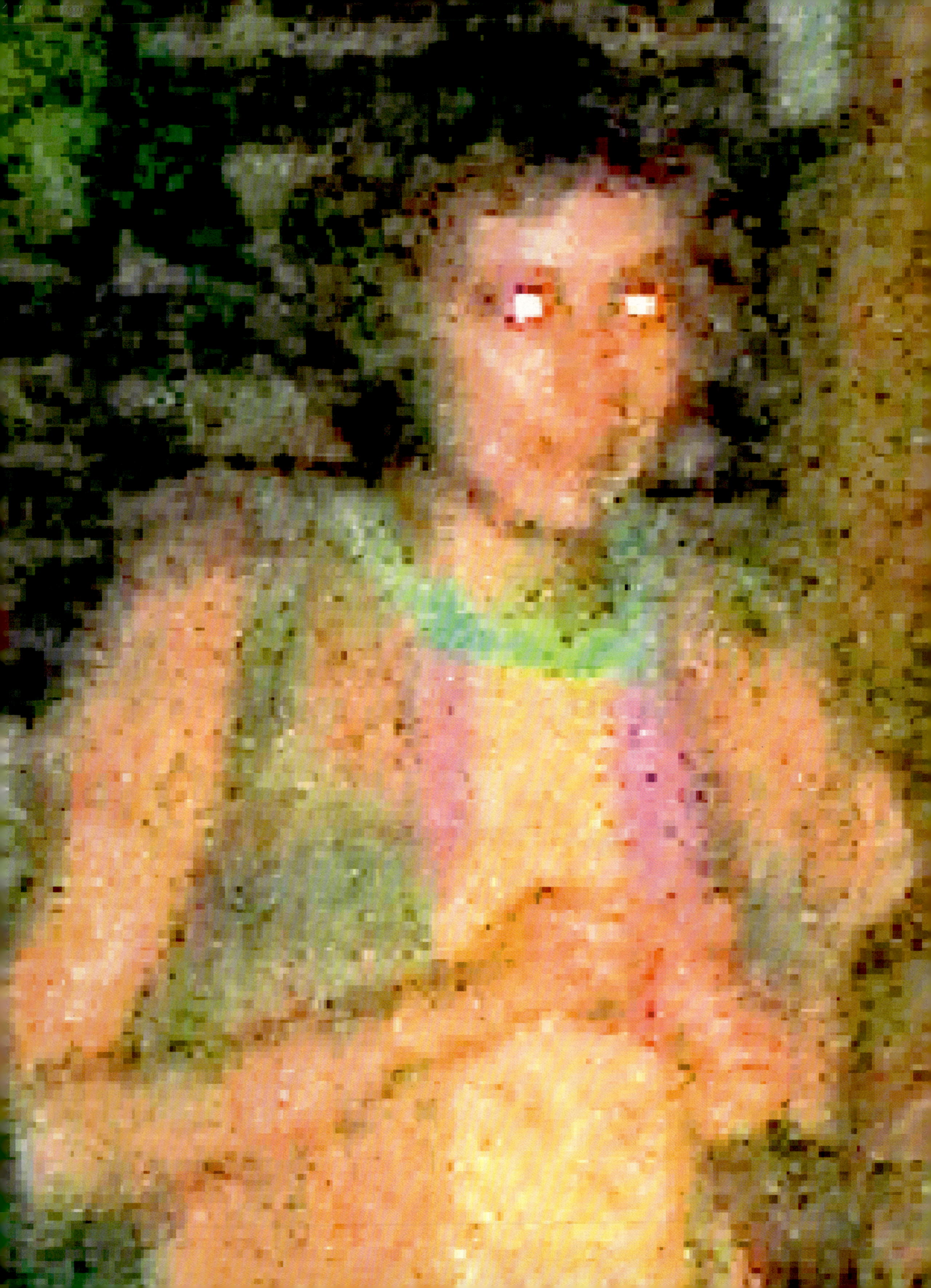

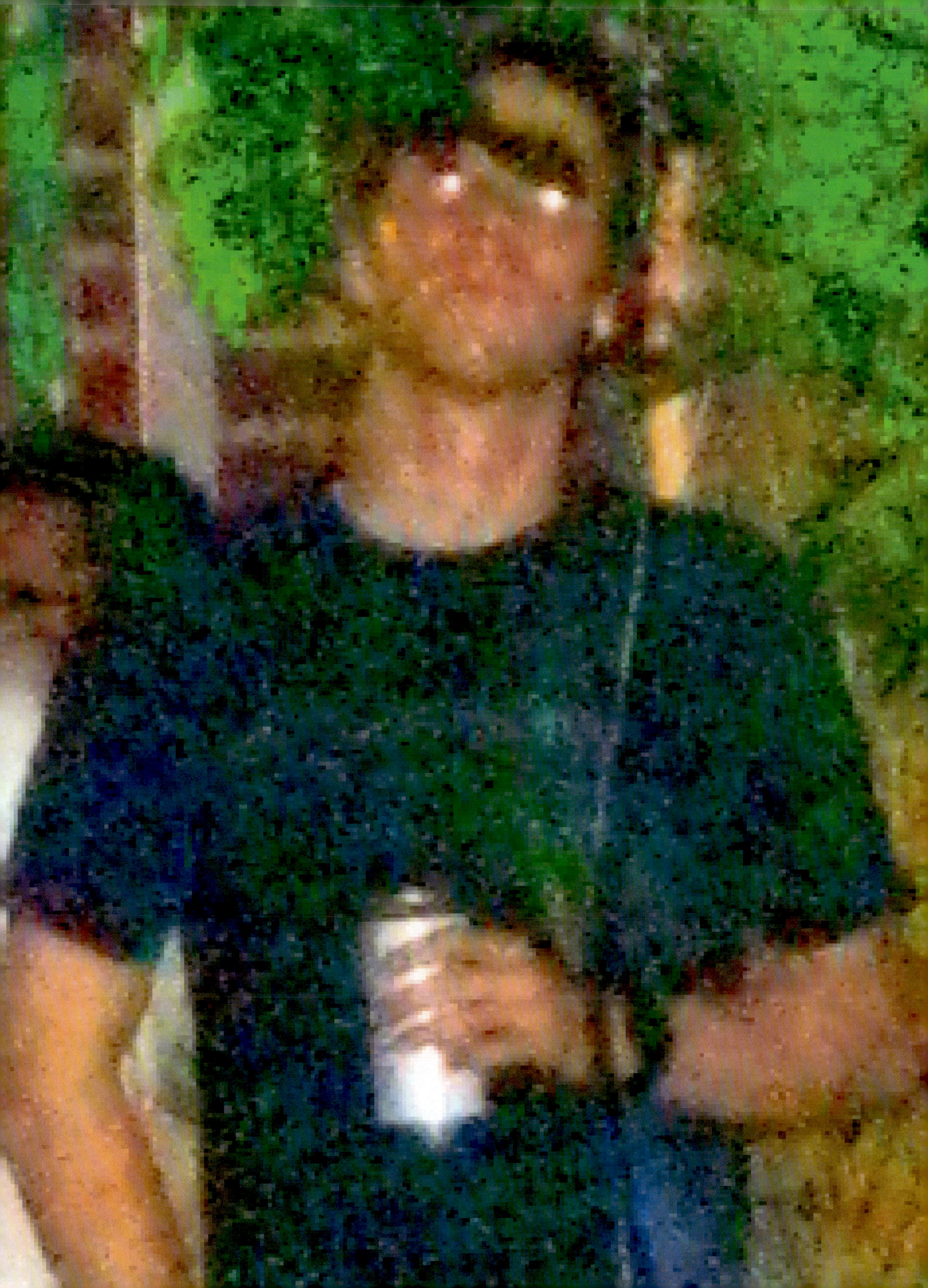

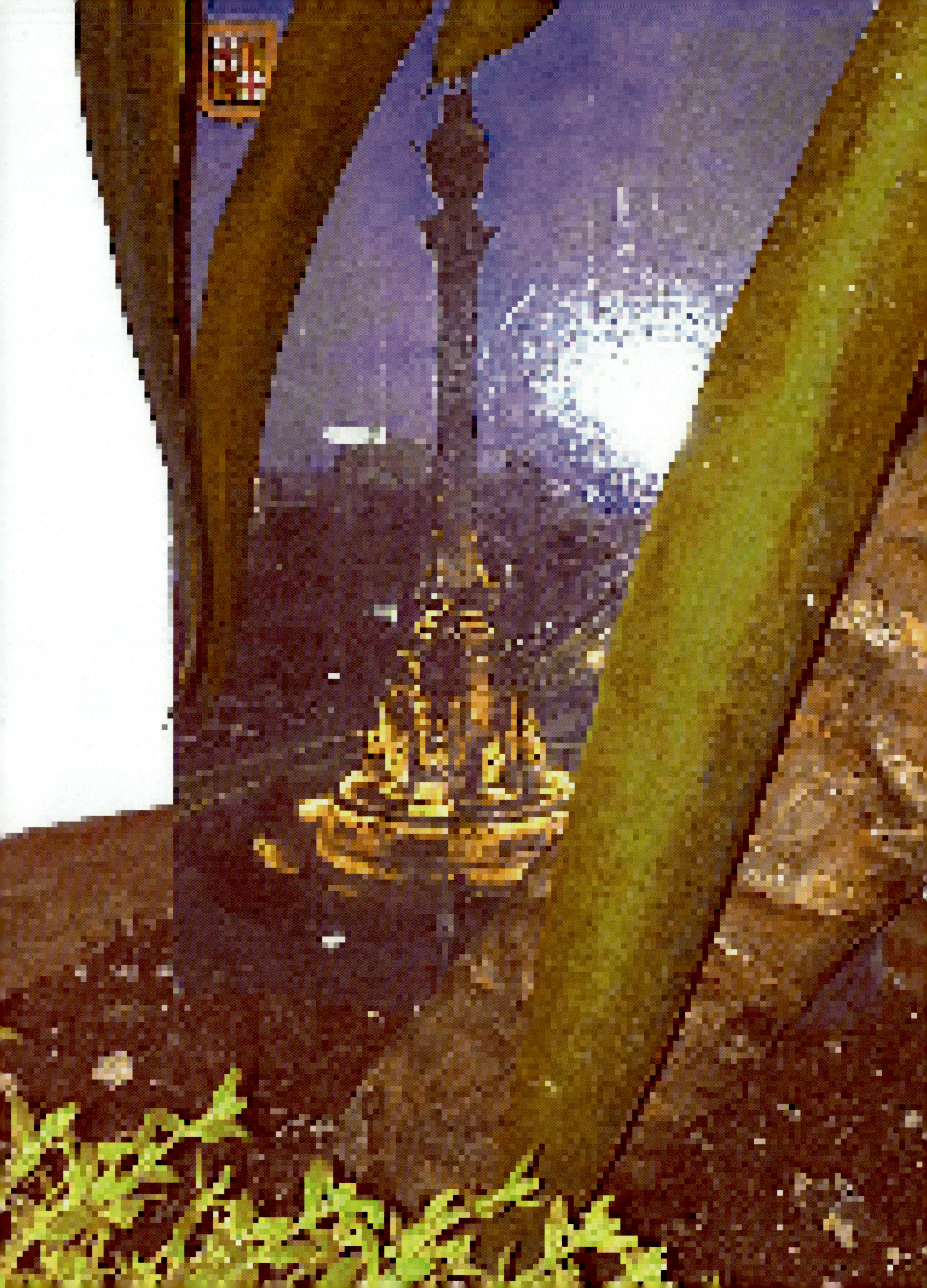

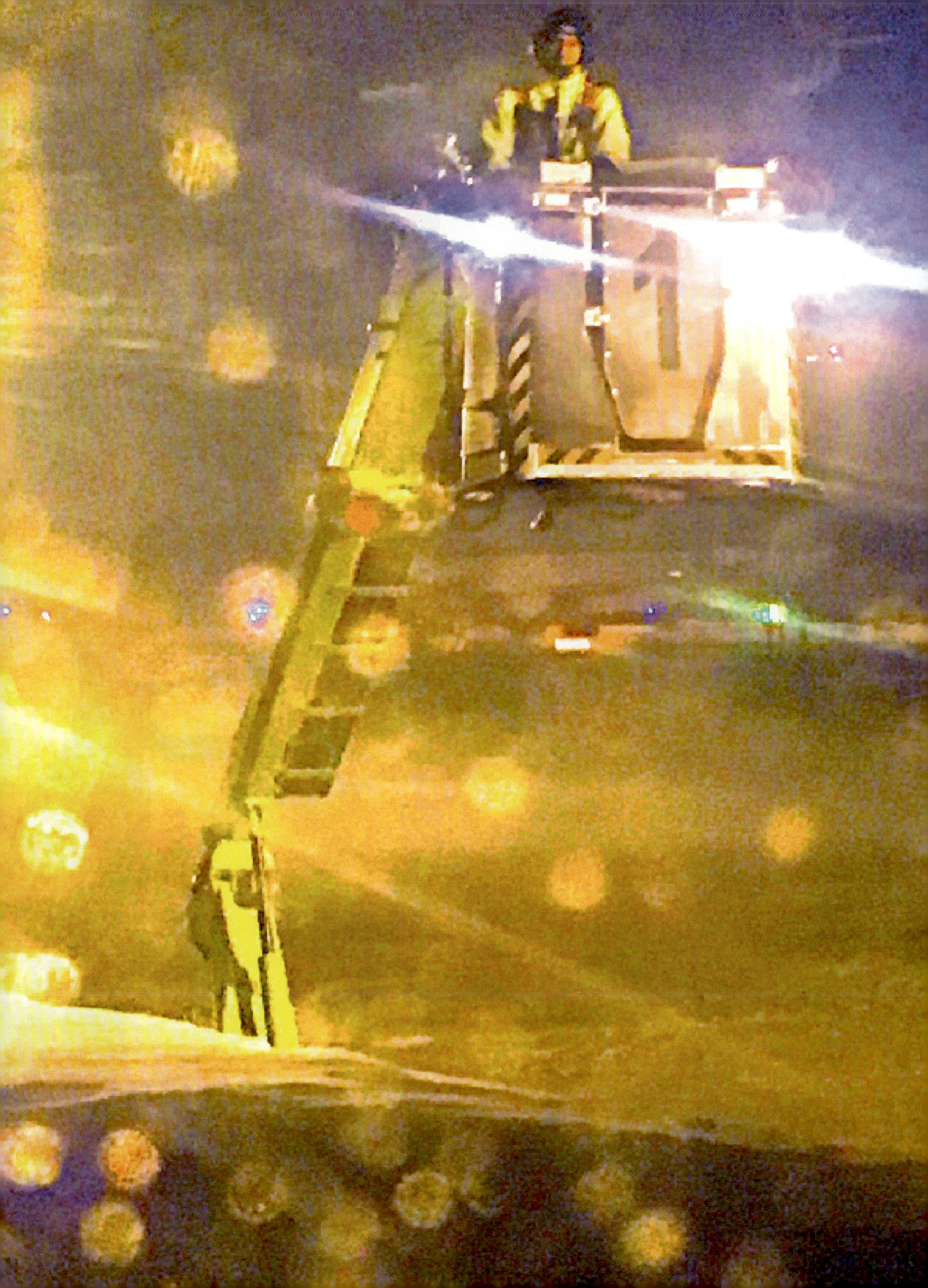

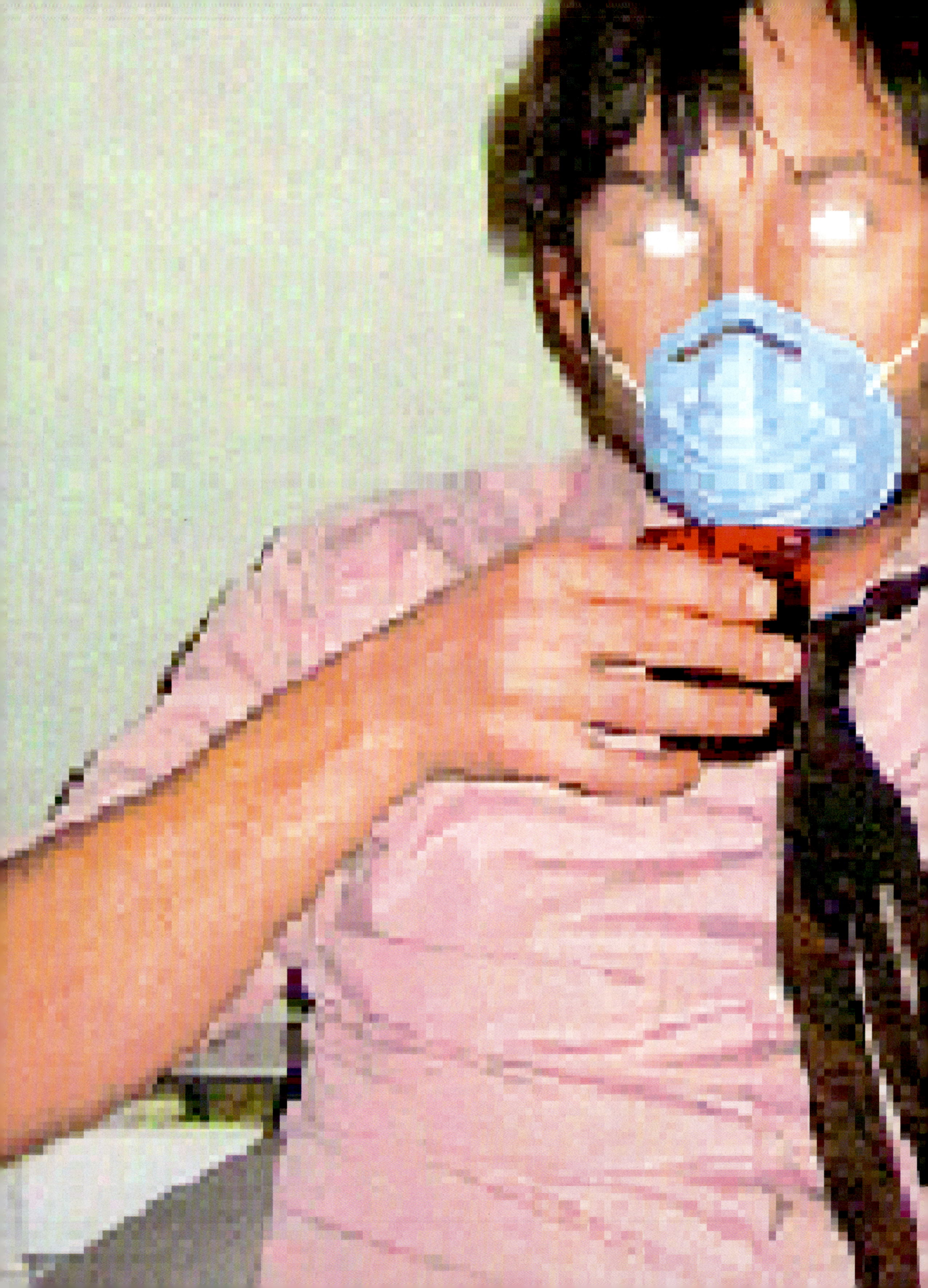

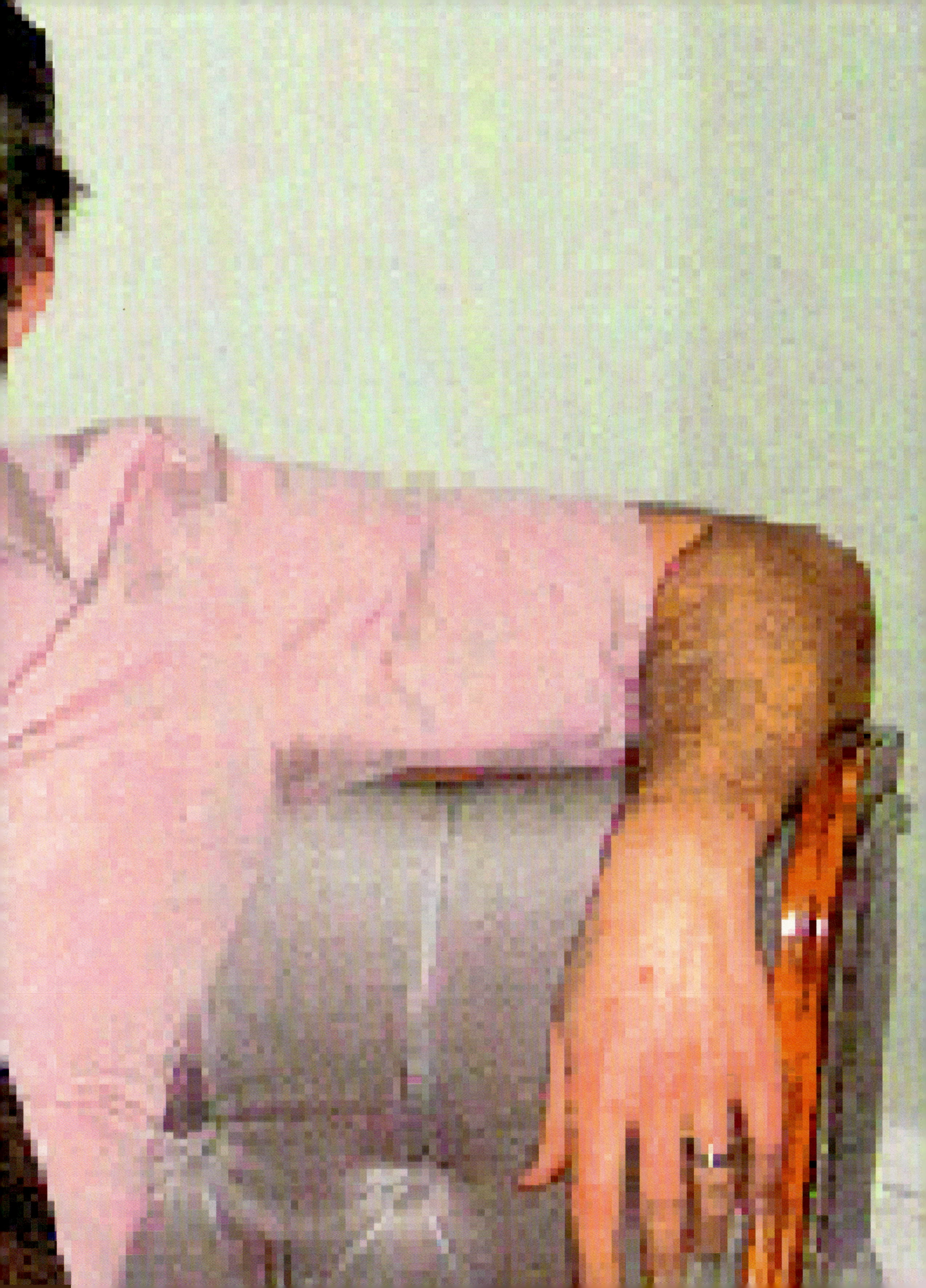

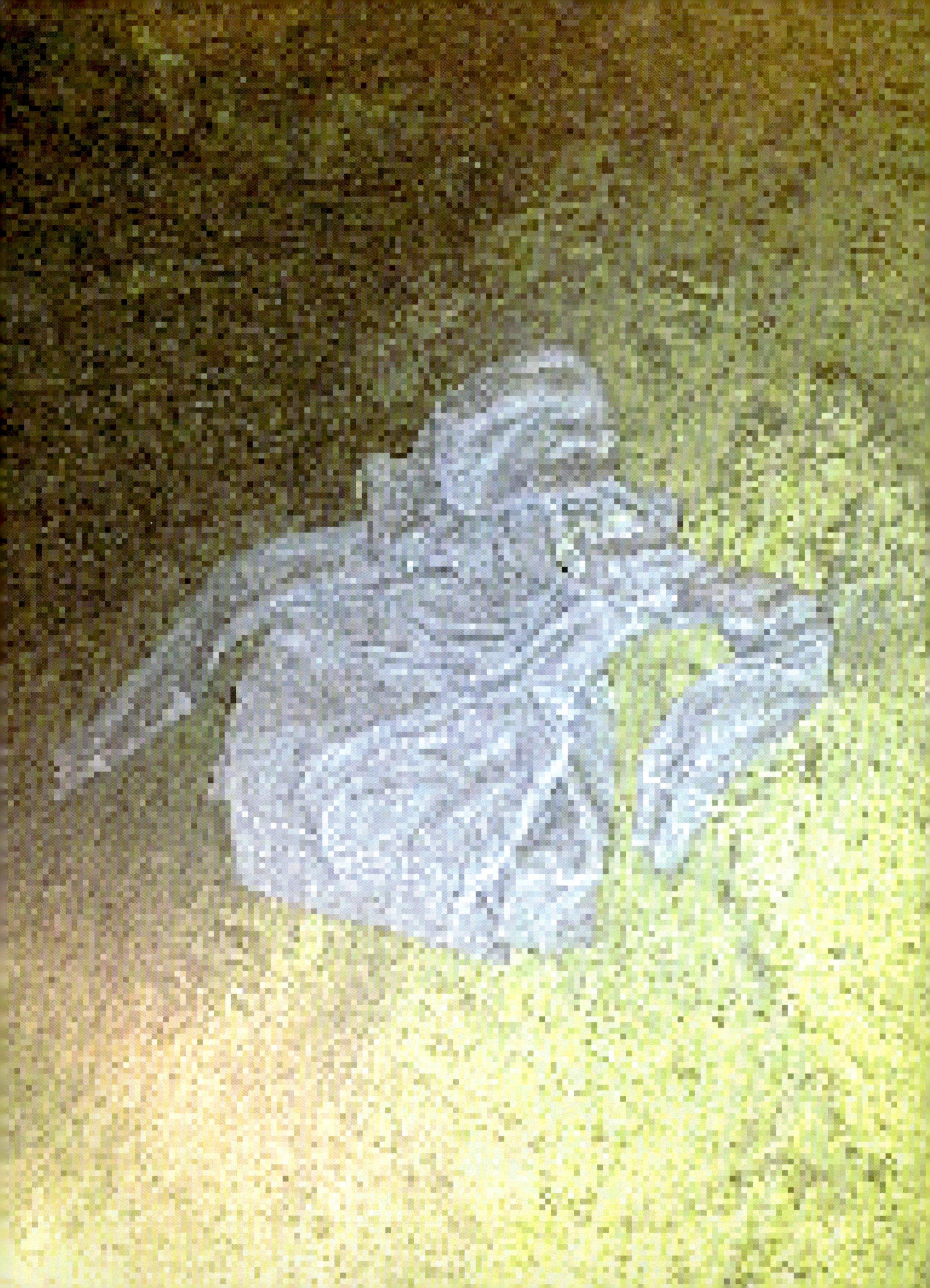

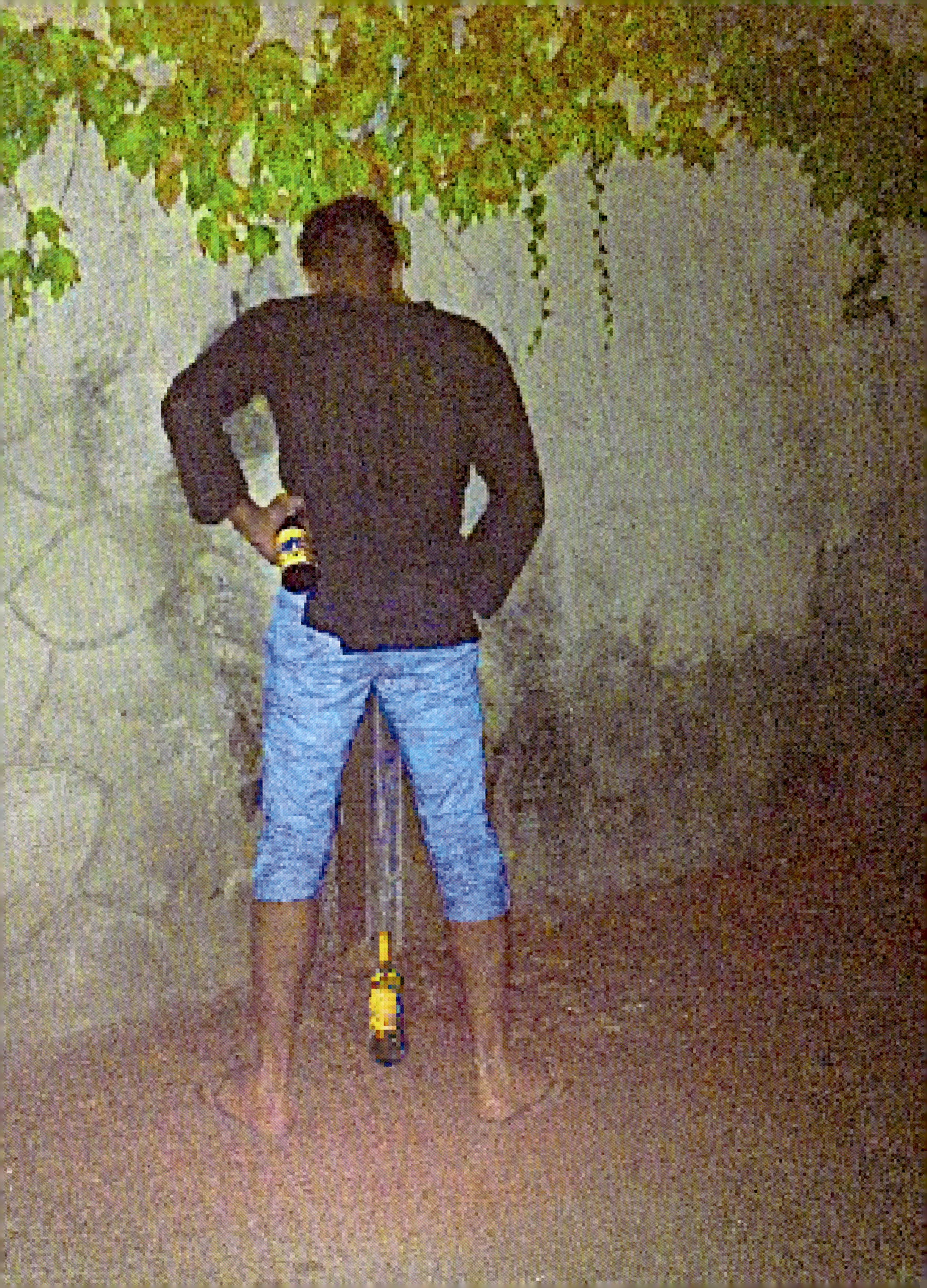

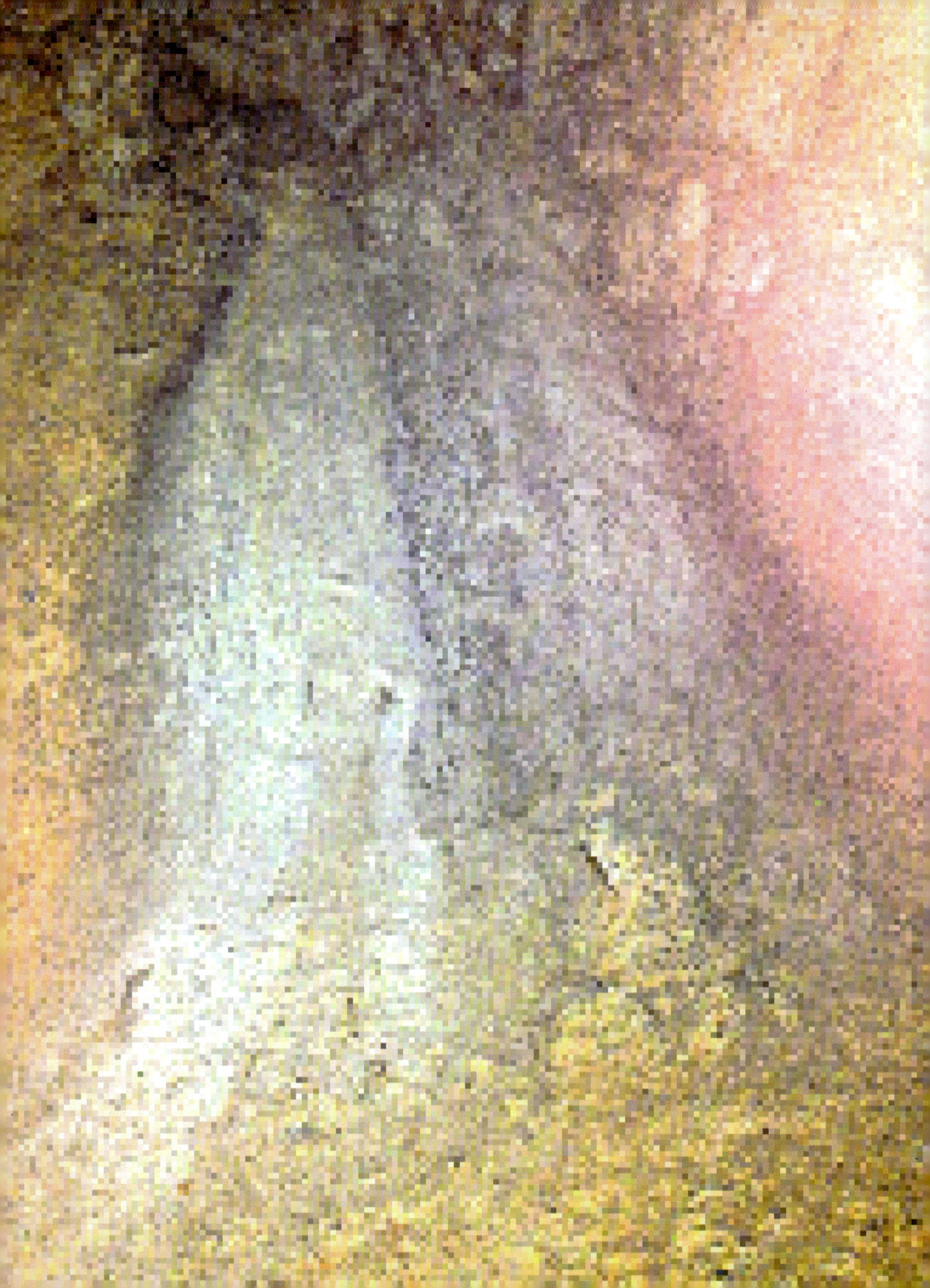

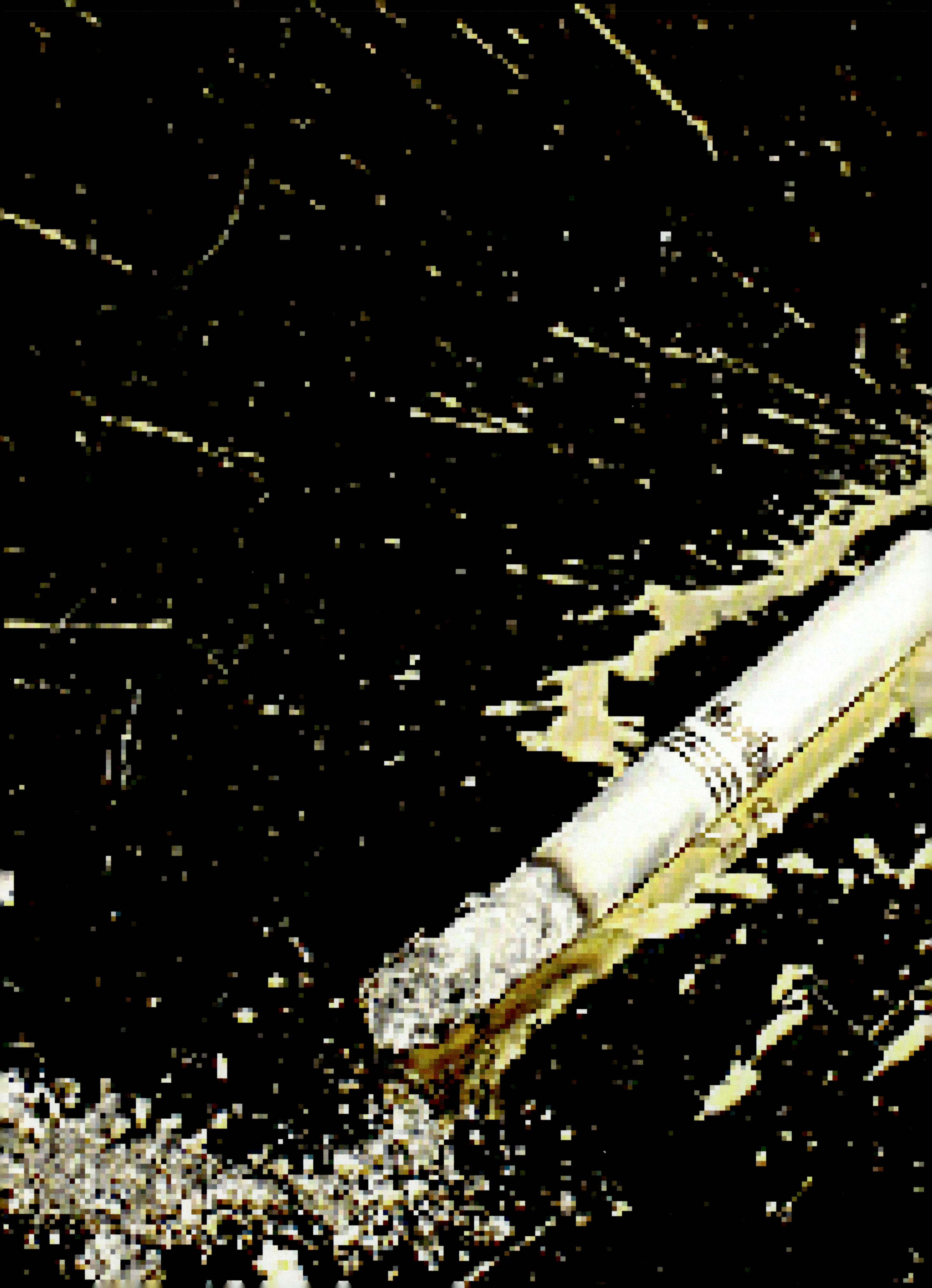

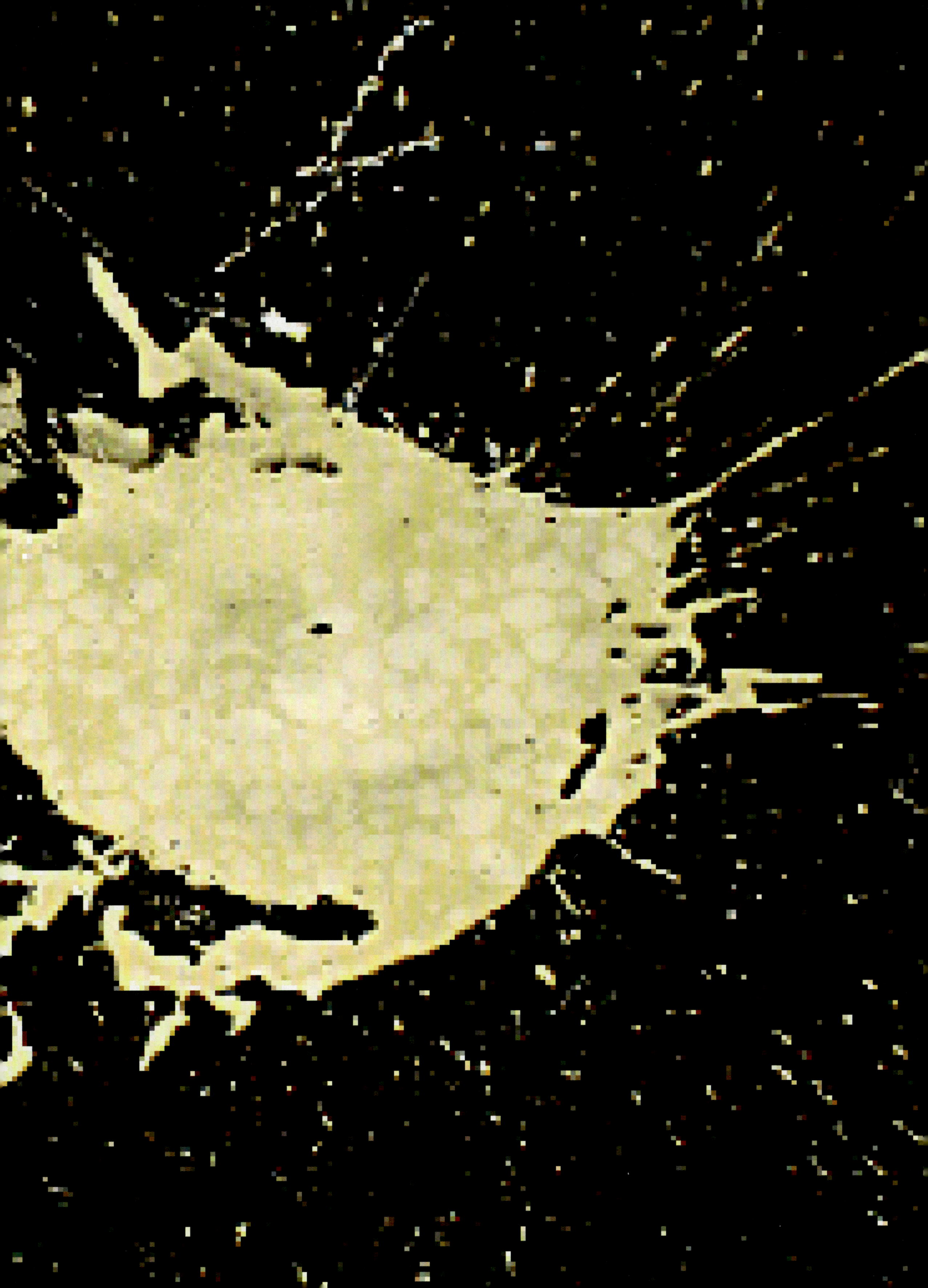

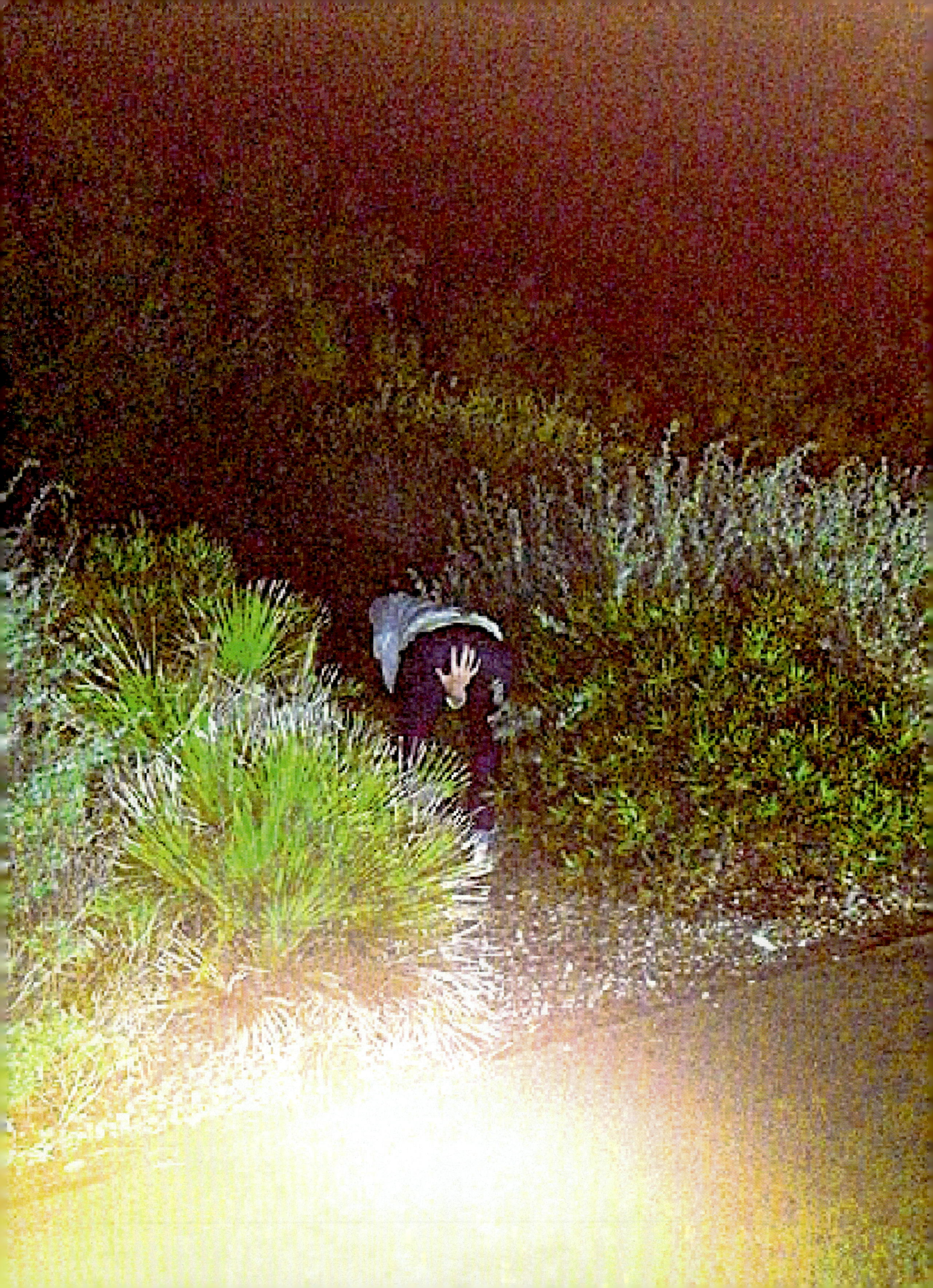

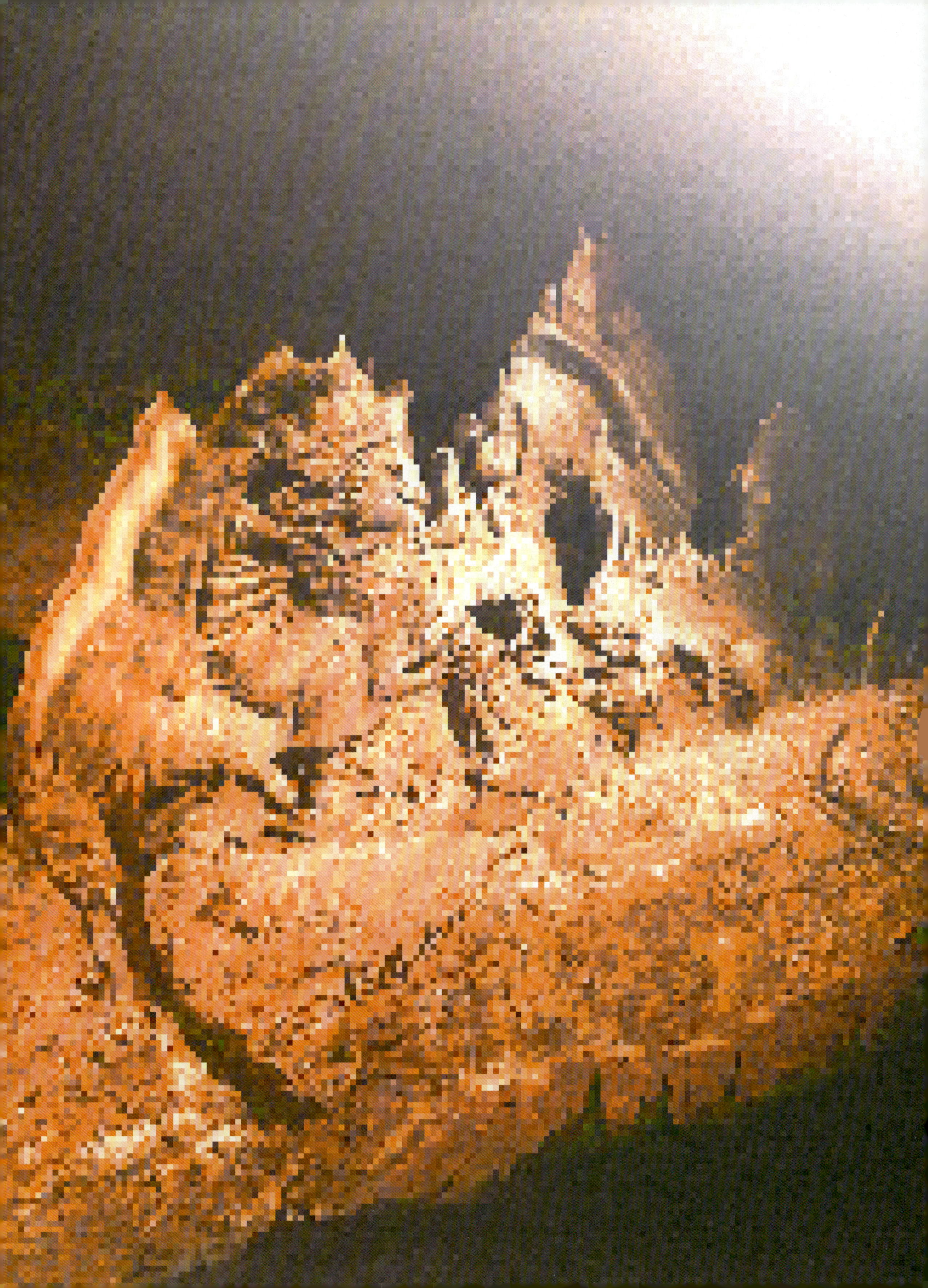

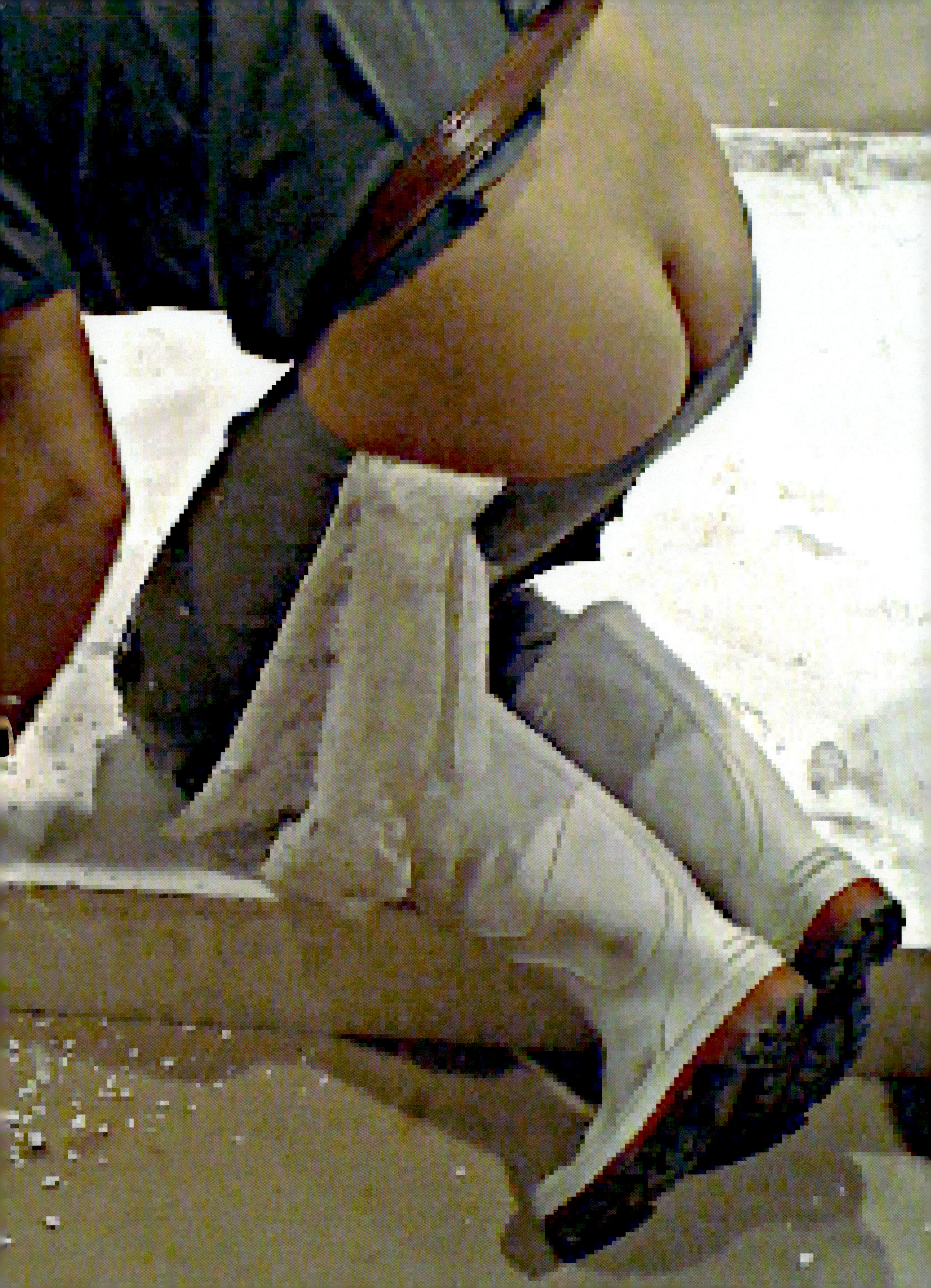

Gabriel Jones took these photographs in M
Brooklyn, Paris and Marseille, between 20
and 2018. The images were taken with va
cameras and aesthetically cropped.

Les photographies de Gabriel Jones ont ét
entre 2004 et 2018, à Montréal, Brooklyn,
et Marseille avec différents appareils num
pour ensuite être recadrées.

Cameras / Appareils : Sony Ericsson W810
Canon Digital IXUS 80 IS, Nikon E500,
Canon PowerShot SD600, Pentax Optio S
Sony DSC-W30, iPhone 3G, 4, 4S, SE.

Ph

Desig
Published wit